Unnaturally Green

Unnaturally Green

one girl's journey along a
yellow brick road less traveled

Felicia Ricci

FLR ❧ Brooklyn, New York

The names and identifying aspects of some characters have been changed. This book is in no way affiliated with or endorsed by *Wicked*.

For Grandma Yola, with love.

ACT ONE.
THE CYCLONE

ৎ৩

GREEN
/grin/ *adjective*

1. having a flavor that is raw, harsh, and acid, due especially to a lack of maturity: *a green teenager.*

2. of the color of growing foliage, between yellow and blue in the spectrum: *a green tree.*

3. simple; unsophisticated; gullible; easily fooled: *a green newcomer.*

4. fresh, recent, or new: *a green relationship.*

5. not fully developed or perfected in growth or condition; unripe; not properly aged: *a green actress.*

1. COME BACKSTAGE

I saw *Wicked* as a surly and disbelieving English major the winter of my sophomore year at Yale University. In my 19 years of living, breathing, and having strong opinions, I'd done dozens of shows, all of which were non-professional and most of which involved jazz hands. When it came to theater—or anything, for that matter—clearly I knew what I was talking about.

My parents were visiting New York from Rhode Island, loading up on shows for their semi-yearly Broadway fix, and I'd taken the train from New Haven to meet them. We had great seats—fifth row, center—and I sat sandwiched between my giddy little sister and bespectacled boyfriend, a small man who now exists as a bust in my Dating History Museum, along with other lifeless renderings of ill-advised suitors.

All right, impress me, I thought from my seat. *I want to see what this hype is all about.*

(**GREEN**. 1. having a flavor that is raw, harsh, and acid, due especially to a lack of maturity: *a green teenager.*)

With a flourish, the show began, and in moments, I felt my tight little sophomore buttocks unclench. Soon, I was hooked:

oohing and *ahhing* at the music, sets, lights, costumes, and performers—just like the millions of fans who had come before me. Most enthralling was the green-skinned protagonist, played by actress Shoshana Bean, a high-cheek-boned goddess with belting and riffing powers that bordered on the supernatural.

Elphaba Thropp was her name. She'd been known first as a villain, as the so-called "Wicked Witch" of *The Wizard of Oz*. Now she was a heroine. Each night at the Gershwin she came to life for thousands of theatergoers. Over time, her story would become a worldwide phenomenon, proliferating into productions that played across the globe, breaking box office records—changing the world, one unclenched sophomore buttock at a time.

I watched as Shoshana tore across the proscenium, clocking the audience with high note after higher note, sailing into the vocal stratosphere, forging through each scene with mind-blowing skill.

Was she human, I wondered, or engineered to make the rest of us feel meek and unworthy? These were legitimate questions, and I needed answers.

It just doesn't seem possible!

I felt like Isaac Newton, watching his beloved gravity apple spontaneously levitate, then tap dance to ragtime music.

Soon it hit me like a (pick your cliché): ton of bricks, speeding truck, Catholic nun. Amidst my awe and disbelief, I had joined the ranks of probably every other girl in the audience.

This is my dream role!

Elphaba Thropp had won me over. She was young. Hopeful. Misunderstood.

Just like me!

Strange in appearance, unwavering in conviction, Elphaba was a heroine for those of us who, at any point in our lives, had felt different.

My next thought? (And I hope you saw this coming.)

I want to play that role.

A stirring ambition for a young English major—soon squelched by the droning voice of reason.

You could never, in a million years.

❖   ❖   ❖

A million years later and I was back in the audience of *Wicked*, making my way through rows of velvet seats at San Francisco's Orpheum Theater, towing along my tiny new friend named Libby. With three minutes until curtain, we shimmied to the center of an aisle, wearing our all-access lanyards, and seated ourselves next to a slouchy couple and a little girl wearing a tiara. From my chair, I felt a gurgle deep in my gut.

Ugh.

I had jolted awake that dreary March Tuesday three hours before my alarm. My stomach had started to churn, like bread dough kneading itself—filled with a sticky clod of anticipation.

Gripping my armrests, I tried to relax.

"This is exciting, isn't it?" said Libby, with a little leg-kick-bounce.

"Yes," I said, meaning no.

Libby wasn't just a spectator; she was also a member of *Wicked*'s cast. As standby (or first understudy) to the role of Glinda, when she wasn't performing she was waiting—sometimes watching the show, sometimes diddling around backstage. Still fresh in my mind was her cutie patootie performance last weekend, when she had stolen audience members' hearts as the charming, beautiful, universally adored Glinda Upland. She had been perfectly cast—a ball of glitter, with platinum hair that framed her button of a blue-eyed face, which, like the rest of her, was doll-sized.

As we burrowed into our red seats, Libby's feet barely touched the floor.

As for me?

I was not doll-sized, but I guess I was moderately adorable—at least more than usual. Tonight I'd taken a break from sweatpants and instead went all *Extreme Makeover* on myself, arriving at the theater in a nautical-inspired blue and white sundress with wedge boots. I'd even attempted a salon blowout, which for me meant flipping my hair upside-down, blasting it with heat, and spritzing it with every bottle under my bathroom sink. The full effect made me look like a longhaired poodle that had accidentally licked an electrical socket. But it was an upgrade from looking like my old kickball coach, with her low-slung pants, messy bun, and chin hairs.

You may be wondering why I, a woman content to look like a gym teacher, would go through so much trouble. Well, you see: I had a new job, and it was my first day.

Drumroll, please.

As of that dreary March Tuesday, despite all reason, logic, and governing laws of the universe, I, Felicia Ricci, was the new Elphaba standby in the San Francisco Company of *Wicked*.

Yep!

Me. The novice. The nobody. The nincompoop.

Was it a joke? By all accounts—no. But, if yes? I was probably the punch line.

Wicked had offered me my first professional theater contract—ever. Before then, it had been 23 years' worth of amateur hour: summer camp, student productions, workshops in basements. In college I hadn't had much formal training, but tried my best to do theater between essay writing. It was a piecemeal fling with the dramatic arts, which soon snowballed from a hobby into the beginnings of a career.

When it came to *Wicked*, I felt a bit like I'd been elected Vice President after having served exclusively on eighth-grade student council.

Seasoned actress Eden Espinosa was my Commander in Chief (or the cast's principal Elphaba) and I was next in line to take over should anything go wrong. You might also think of me as a member of the Secret Service, "Worthy of Trust and Confidence," enlisted to throw myself in the line of fire.

March 30, 2010—the night in question (stomach of dough, poodle hair)—was my first night on call for duty.

Four days before I'd had my only dress rehearsal, or "put-in," when everybody else in the cast performed in street clothes and I strutted around in full costume, feeling like I'd seriously overdressed for a party. But this was a welcomed upgrade, since before that I'd been practicing the show alone, chattering away as Elphaba to my imaginary friends like a happy schizophrenic.

As Elphaba, "full costume" meant having my face, ears, neck, and hands slathered in layers of green makeup. I stared in the mirror, transfixed, as I watched *Wicked*'s makeup designer wave his wide Japanese brush like a magic wand, turning me from pallid yellow to bright emerald, as the lines and blemishes on my skin surrendered to the smooth contours of my now unrecognizable face. Next, there were wigs, one for each act, topped by a series of hats, under which there were laid two, sometimes three body microphones. Last was a green mesh jumpsuit, a skin-tight sheath for my arms and chest that was like connective tissue between wardrobe and makeup—nightmare to those who, like me, are blessed with healthy and abundant sweat glands.

When the curtain fell on my put-in, I'd earned the stamp of Approved Standby from the *Wicked* creative team. This stamp was less "100% Perfect" and more "Good Enough," but that was all right—I knew I'd have lots more rehearsal and coaching in the coming weeks. I liked to think of myself as a little green Elphaba tree—potted with soil, but not yet pruned.

(**GREEN**. 2. of the color of growing foliage, between yellow and blue in the spectrum: *a green tree*.)

In the meantime, I would have to do my best.

The lights dimmed and a hush fell over the crowd, like we were straining to hear a secret. There was a blast of horns as *Wicked*'s opening number began, its company of Ozian villagers, swathed in clothes of unusual texture and proportion, cheering and throwing streamers to celebrate the death of Elphaba, infamous Wicked Witch of the West.

As the sight and sound extravaganza flickered across the stage, I sank into my chair, until I was the approximate height of Libby. I rested my hands in my lap and closed my eyes.

This shouldn't be too hard, I thought to myself.

The truth? Despite my anxiety, there was no *real* reason to be nervous. Not today. Being the newest agent to *Wicked*'s Secret Service, I was primed for combat—but it would be a rare and distant day that I'd take a bullet for the president.

It was even possible I would *never* play Elphaba. Between starring in *Wicked* on Broadway, then opening the Los Angeles company, talent powerhouse Eden Espinosa had racked up many years of experience before swooping into San Francisco. Since arriving last month she hadn't called out once, and each week had conquered all eight shows with Napoleonic tenacity.

This was quite rare for actresses playing Elphaba, I was told, since the role was so grueling. But Eden was a force to be reckoned with. In light of her flawless spree, when I walked into work in my nautical-inspired sundress, stage manager David welcomed me to my "first day of guitar lessons," what with all the free time I would have as standby.

Just relax.

I opened my eyes. Kendra Kassebaum, our Glinda, had arrived onstage via mechanical "bubble," descending from the fly space to walk and greet the Ozians. Libby, low in her seat, stared, entranced, studying Kendra's every move as she swept from end to end in her blue shimmering gown, as she had done hundreds of times before.

Minutes later, Eden dashed onstage, front and center, a green halo surrounding her from head to boot, showing us all, especially me, what it meant to be a star. Soon it was time for her first song, "The Wizard and I," which involved all kinds of high, gutsy belting, second only in difficulty to one other Elphaba song, "Defying Gravity," which happened at the end of Act I.

Eden was every kind of confident, infusing the role of Elphaba with a passion that had, for years, made audiences thump their Playbills like Holy Bibles. I'd spent hours scouring YouTube for bootlegs of Eden, each of which gave me full-on body tingles. I'd even studied her performance for inspiration before my own *Wicked* audition.

Now I'm her standby, I thought, in a daze.

I sighed conclusively, feeling myself calming. With Eden at the helm, there was nothing to worry about. If the Big Day ever arrived, I'd have loads of time to practice.

No, not today.

Finally Eden was in the home stretch of the song, singing about the breadth of her limitless future, crossing downstage to center, reaching her arms from side to side. She planted her feet, winding up for the vocal finale.

Then, it happened.

There was a wobble, a momentary *blip* in the stream of sound. She slipped slightly under pitch, and there was a grating noise rising in her throat. After taking a deep breath, she forged to the final note, a C above Middle C—which rests smack in the middle of female singers' *passagios*, or vocal breaks. It seemed that Eden had something in her throat—phlegm or a swollen gland—that kept tripping up her cords.

I shifted in my chair.

"Don't worry," whispered Libby, "she's got it."

Midway through the note Eden's voice stopped completely, like a phone line that had suddenly gone dead. The orchestra raced to the end of the underscoring as Eden swung her arms over her head, a choreographed gesture to mark the end of the song. As she moved through the silence, spinning with momentum, her prop glasses flew off to stage left, a peg bursting from the self-destructing machine.

Instantly the lights changed and the orchestra cut away, as Eden strode to stage left, scooping up her glasses.

Ending its momentary calm, my stomach had begun to braid itself into a Challah loaf, twisting and turning, bubbling with the ravenous yeast of anxiety.

Was Eden sick? Or was it a fluke?

According to *Wicked*'s sequence of scenes, she would have to stay onstage for two more songs. Then, once she exited, she could decide whether to continue performing or—

The unthinkable!

I was gripping my armrests, like a passenger on a nose-diving airplane. How many minutes before I hit the ground?

Speak words of comfort to me, Libby!

"Maybe you should take out your phone," she said.

"What?" I hissed. "Are you serious?"

"Just in case," she said.

No, not today.

I looked up. Eden was gone.

And now a lecture excerpt from Life Lessons 101, a class I keep flunking and having to repeat.

LL101: **You can't always plan. The universe may intervene.**

Apparently, I'm supposed to accept this fact—that the universe can do whatever it wants. Kind of like how my mother would steal into my childhood room and rearrange my books and toys against my will.

"When you're on your own, you can have everything the way you like," she'd say.

When will that day come? I always wondered.

That night in the Orpheum, in the red velvet seats, an incoming text from the stage manager buzzed the answer: *no, not today.*

David: 8:40 PM hello there – come backstage – she is not sure she is going to stay in. we will know more soon

Oh my God.

I hustled from the audience through the "personnel only" doors, saying a silent prayer that I'd either:

A) Not actually have to go on.

B) Not actually have to go on.

There really was no second option.

My gait was stiff and hulking, my lanyard swinging back and forth from my neck, a pendulum ticking toward my worst fate. I followed Libby as she scampered ahead with tiny rapid strides through the stairwells and crossovers.

Just breathe.

We emerged at the left end of the upstage curtain, steps away from Eden's dressing room, where I saw stage manager David speaking in low tones to our company manager. They spun around to face us, their expressions contorting into broad, unflinching smiles, which was especially alarming to see on David, who reminded me of a wax figure.

I tried to speak, but formed less an English word than the sound of a dying pigeon.

Libby stepped in. "What's the deal?"

"You're on!" David said to me, his smile so big it practically looped around his neck.

"Oh, right," I said, as all of my body went numb.

"I told you stuff like this happens," he said.

"No, you said, 'Welcome to your first day of guitar lessons.'"

He ignored this.

"You've got fifteen minutes before we're sending you on."

David knocked on Eden's door and together the four of us swept in, where we were greeted by many others: the wig guy, the makeup guy, the Elphaba dresser, and Eden herself, still in costume, spraying liquid vocal coat into her mouth.

"Sorry about this, girl," she said to me.

"Oh, no problem," I said, because it was opposite day.

Even so:

Worthy of Trust and Confidence, I will do my duty!

Inside, everything was unfamiliar; Eden's clothes, makeup, humidifiers, and souvenir paraphernalia were scattered about the room, and I wasn't sure how to make my first move without toppling the figurative Jenga tower. Instead of heading anywhere with purpose, I did a kind of side-step to the center of the room, like a polite, disoriented crab.

Kathleen, the Elphaba dresser, spoke first.

"Here are your undergarments and leotard."

As I grabbed them, I wondered if I was supposed to change in front of everyone, as a kind of spectator sport, but decided to retreat into the adjacent bathroom as Kathleen called out to me,

"You're running on mid-Emerald City, so it'll be the black dress with kneepads. And at least we'll avoid the quick change!"

"Right!" I yelled back, as if I knew what she was talking about.

The bathroom was cramped, but spacious enough for a swift clothes-off, clothes-on maneuver. Thanks to years of performing in under-funded, under-staffed, and under-rehearsed amateur theater, I had become awesome at multitasking under pressure. In peak form, I could vocalize in modulating scales while also curling my hair, brushing my teeth, shaving my legs in the sink, and texting between one and five people.

I emerged from the bathroom seconds later, fully decked in the most unflattering ensemble possible: opaque black tights rolled all the way up to my bust—like charred casing on an overstuffed hot dog—black knee pads, black lace boots, and a black bra. If you saw me out of context you'd think I was preparing for some kind of dominatrix roller derby.

The makeup designer spoke next, in dulcet, soothing tones. "Have a seat," he cooed.

I plunked down in the makeup chair, ready to surrender to the engulfing swatches of green.

"Here, take this brush and start painting your hands and neck," he said.

"Okay," I slurred back.

God. Look at me.

It was near impossible to perform this hand-eye coordinated task while floating outside my own body, but I did my best, watching the wig guy in the mirror as he joined in the spectacle, coiling my poodle blowout into pin-curl loops, pressing them down onto my head, while I slathered myself in green like a preschooler who'd been told she could paint on the walls.

In a flash I was transported back—back to my first brush with spontaneous theater disaster—which happened during an elementary school production of (no joke) *The Wizard of Oz*, when my hand-sewn Cowardly Lion jumpsuit fell apart onstage. Right after "If I Only Had the Nerve," as I was confessing fear of my lion's tail to Dorothy, the damn thing came off in my hands, dangling from my feeble fourth-grade grip, like a furry, lifeless snake. Committed to staying in the moment, I turned to Dorothy and shouted, "You killed my tail!" at which point I threw it at her.

This set a precedent for the rest of my theater stints: if anything went wrong, my right brain would just take over, without my consent, and dictate that I would do something—anything—to keep the action rolling. This happened again during a high school dance recital, when I forgot the entire second half of our jazz routine and so started free-styling as 1970s John Travolta. The other girl was stunned and stopped dancing completely, which meant that in the end everybody thought *she* had messed up— and that our choreographer had really weird taste.

Tonight, I wondered, horrified, would John Travolta make an encore performance?

And all of Oz was stricken with Saturday Night Fever.

Stage manager David asked if I had any last-minute questions—*any last requests?*—then next assured me everything was going to be fine, which of course was a lie. I said something back to him, but I have no idea what it was—I was too busy thinking, "I hope I don't get the hiccups and start farting uncontrollably," which guaranteed that this would, indeed, happen. Even worse, for the life of me I couldn't remember if I'd warmed up my voice that day—and, holy crap, I wasn't sure I could even *sing* the damn part!

How will I ever be able to do this?

There were supposed to be hours more rehearsal before I'd ever go on. What happened to more practice? What happened to more coaching? What happened to pruning my Elphaba tree?

Universe, you're such a pain in my ass!

I'd been painted, primed, and preened, and the hydra that was my assembly team dispersed so that I might stand at full stature, dressed in black from head to toe. There I stood, frozen, the final frame in my own version of one of those evolution posters, in which the chimp becomes the human. The Felicia had become The Elphaba: newly-green skin, pointy witch's hat pinned to her rather large head—a head that should have belonged to someone else—someone older, wiser, and better equipped to rescue a multimillion dollar musical.

Just breathe.

Somebody handed me a water bottle, so I gulped. Somebody handed me green glasses, so I put them on. Through the dressing room monitor playing live audio I could hear we were minutes from the swap—the moment when Eden would run off stage and I would run on, hopefully without anyone in the audience noticing.

We began our trek to the wings. Every image whizzed by, like scenery past a runaway train—with green-tinted windows. Though surrounded by people, I felt so inconsolably alone, trying to ignore the chatter of voices in my head. I needed to release myself from the stronghold of self-doubt and become someone else entirely.

To become Elphaba Thropp, brave and uncompromising.

2. AUDITION

The casting office, large with high ceilings, was like an airport terminal. Here, travelers dawdled in limbo, helpless to their fates. When it came time to board, so came it time to pray, breathless, that they wouldn't crash into the side of a mountain.

I sat on a bench, examining the walls. The far section was painted green. Not a calming, earthy green; a neon, seizure-inducing green—like 80s spandex or radioactive waste. The other wall had five identical doors, each of which opened to a different room, like a funhouse that was not fun. Next to every door was a table with a sign-up sheet and clusters of people organized by size, gender, and color—the short balding men, the muscular Hispanic teenagers, then, in the distance, a cheerleader squad of blonde girls wearing Keds and doing calf stretches. Every now and then somebody would come out one of the doors, looking stunned and confused, like they'd just awoken from a nightmare-filled nap.

Seizure-funhouse-terminal or not, this was better than most audition studios, which, if pressed on the matter, I would bet were designed by the same people who designed prisons, what with their barred windows, cell-sized rooms, and torture-chamber bathrooms. This jailhouse aesthetic was something you noticed at first, but eventually got used to—like the smell of sewage, or the fact that your high school boyfriend clearly preferred men. After a year of auditioning in the city, if ever I changed clothes in a stall larger than a dog kennel, while liquid didn't drip soundlessly from the ceiling onto my head, I thought it the absolute height of extravagance.

I'd arrived at today's audition fifteen minutes early, allotting time at home for a hot shower warm-up and the consumption of my audition breakfast of choice: a banana, to be eaten precisely one hour before my appointment. Months of testing and I'd determined that this was the perfect actor's food and time frame to eat in; you could gear up for your appointment with adequate energy stores, and not worry that you'd have to—you know. Go number two. (TMI? Get used to it—this is a memoir!) Not only that, but I'd read online that bananas decreased bloating, a helpful perk when you're trying to squeeze into something form-fitting and/or convince a casting panel of the fake weight you've listed on your resume.

To keep myself occupied, I started leafing through my audition materials—all twenty-six pages. It wasn't long before my fingers started sticking to the paper, smudging ink and crinkling the corners. Sweaty hands could mean only one thing, so I glanced down at my pits to check for leakage. Sure enough, two dark stains had begun to creep down the sides of my rib cage, like the careful work of pit-soldiers digging secret sweat-trenches. Panicked, I nose-dove into myself for a whiff, relieved to find that there was no discernible stench. Yet.

Publicly smelling one's own armpits is generally bad form; at auditions, it's a matter of course. Glancing around the room, I saw ten or so other girls engaging in all kinds of fantastically weird behavior. Some were hunched over and swaying, others were reciting lines with their eyes closed or humming softly to themselves. One shoeless girl was blowing raspberries while shimmying and slapping her own arms. Another sat with a rolling suitcase and kept applying lipstick, blotting her lips, tucking her lipstick into her suitcase, looking up, then reaching back for more lipstick. About five loops in, she looked up and I smiled and did a half-wave. The loop kept going, so I said,

"You here for *Wicked*?"

"Yes," she said, reaching for her lipstick.

"Oh, cool! Me too."

She replied with a blot, so I added, for good measure, "That's so fun."

When I'm nervous, conversation is my coping mechanism; ask any doctor who's tried drawing my blood. Growing up I actually loved taking standardized tests, not just because I could overachieve in measurable amounts but because while taking them I was always at my most social. One time before the SAT our proctor was late showing up, so I organized an impromptu game of Two Truths and a Lie, which, by happy accident, helped prime me for the multiple choice section.

Lipstick Loop was clearly not interested in talking to me, so I went back to my materials. Having memorized my lines, I felt fairly confident about the acting portion. But the singing? The excerpt from "The Wizard and I" was bad, and "Defying Gravity" was brutal. Even running the melodies in my head made my vocal cords pulse.

I'd practiced for hours, but the working plan at that point was to "fake it." I wasn't entirely sure what that meant, but I'd heard other actors say it a lot. I think it meant that I should walk in, project a confident version of myself, and under no circumstances start weeping uncontrollably. As if to say, "Ignore the pit stains, ignore the goose honking, and cast me! I'll knock this role out of the park!"

In other words: lie.

Through Un-Funhouse Door 2 I heard the sustained sound of a woman scream-crying. Either that or she was doing an excellent job singing "Defying Gravity." It was hard to tell. This was just one of many perception-bending tricks of audition waiting rooms. Through a closed door, everybody sounds amazing, or at least better than you. I could tell other people's ears were perking up to the shrill (or maybe pleasant?) note that was being held for what seemed like five minutes. Then there was a riff, more scream-crying, another riff, and sudden silence. (Had she keeled over?)

A dark-complexioned woman wearing skinny jeans walked out the door. The scream-crier was in our midst, and I watched as she wagged her mouth and flicked her tongue against the back of her teeth, like there was taffy stuck to her palate. Her hair looked disheveled and I think she was panting a little.

One of the balding men looked up at her.

"Fierce," he said.

Then, as if she didn't hear him, said it again. "*Fierce!*"

Closely behind her was casting director Craig, who was consulting the sign-up sheet.

"Maryann?"

A tiny girl wearing a headband and a poofy wool sweater bounced over to the door.

"You ready?" Craig asked.

She nodded. I watched as she disappeared into the room, an innocent lamb marching to her slaughter. The door closed and soon muffled music started to play.

I was pretty sure I was next, but I tiptoed up to the sign-up sheet to double check. I did this also to position myself closer to the door, for more effective eavesdropping. In oblong cursive, I saw my name etched on the damning document, directly below Maryann's. Next to it was a box for my cell number and union affiliation, the latter of which I'd left blank. Giving the sheet a quick rundown, I saw that almost all the other girls were members of Actor's Equity, which wasn't the end of the world, but maybe a point against me.

Sigh.

To me, being without an Actor's Equity card meant I hadn't yet proven myself. Not to the casting office, not to *Wicked*, and not to myself. I wasn't—by anyone's standards—a "professional." Chugging along the audition circuit for almost a year, I'd created a pressure-cooker situation: no matter how many shows I did, until I'd joined the union and worked under Equity contract, I wouldn't feel like I'd really arrived. Like I'd really become an *actress*.

I leaned in toward the door to listen, immediately regretting it. This girl's voice was perfect. She was nearing the climax of the song, and her delivery was clear and effortless, as if the notes, high and brutal as they were, were floating from her mouth like gossamer bubbles of sound. Dear Maryann had managed to make an incredibly taxing song sound like a lullaby. A stern lullaby— sung by a militant nanny. But a lullaby, nonetheless.

There was some muffled talking, which I assumed meant they were running the scenes. It occurred to me that I should probably start readying my materials. Between a headshot, résumé, binder of songs, and loose sheets of Elphaba music and scene excerpts, it was crucial that I walk into the room with a handle on everything, lest I hand my pianist my headshot and the casting director my water bottle, or a tampon, or something bizarre like this. (You laugh, but it could happen.)

Maryann began a second lullaby, this time to the tune of "Defying Gravity," which meant I had about one minute until my name was called. I felt my teeth start to chatter, my jaw buzzing from the waves of nerves.

Soon the door swung open and Maryann trotted out. Moments later and Craig was standing in front of me.

"Felicia?"

"Yes?"

"Hi, good to see you. You ready?"

"I think so!"

"I'll take your headshot and résumé."

"Awesome."

Then, into the fire!

Through Un-Funhouse Door 2 I soldiered to the center of the room, facing casting director Craig. He had seated himself behind a table, next to a young man in a flannel button-down with a very stylish faux hawk. They were both looking down.

The top of any audition can be awkward, so I like to greet everybody first rather than jump into the material. But if I'm feeling particularly nervous, I sometimes resort to coughing or sneezing, or making some other bodily noise that declares my existence (so far, it hasn't come to farting).

I coughed.

Nothing.

I pointed a finger gun at Faux Hawk.

"Hello there!"

Craig looked up.

"Hello, Felicia. Let's start with 'The Wizard and I.'"

"Great! I've got that right here!"

I walked over to the pianist at the far end of the room.

"Howdy," I said, continuing the Western theme and handing off my sheet music.

"Oh, no need for that," the pianist said, tapping two fingers on his binder, which was overflowing with sheet music. Flustered, I shuffled a bunch of pages to the bottom of my pile, careful to separate my scene excerpts from the rest, sorting each page, one-by-one.

"Whenever you're ready," said Craig.

I tossed my pages on top of the piano and darted back to center.

Help.

Without warning, music began to play—a dreamlike vamp of rolling chords.

I took a deep breath and opened my mouth to sing.

"Unlimited..."

❖   ❖   ❖

I got the call about my *Wicked* audition one frigid December night while I was clawing around in the backseat of a cab.

This wasn't by choice. I was on my way to opening night of *Hee-Haw*, a disaster of a production I had agreed to perform in, whose theater was in the farthest, most deserted corner of lower Manhattan. Since it took an hour and a half to get there by subway, I'd been commuting in taxis, or as I affectionately called them, "dressing rooms that move," prepping for each performance on the way. In so doing, I'd achieved astounding new heights of dexterity, cutting things down to the wire, and flashing many, many pedestrians.

This particular night, it so happened I had almost sealed my eyes shut, trying to glue on an old pair of fake eyelashes. Gripping them with both hands, I gave one final *yank* and ripped the ratty buggers off my lids, along with patches of hair and skin.

The clock read 7:51 p.m., so I had nine minutes to finish my makeup, tease my hair, put on my corset, pencil skirt, and thigh-highs, and get to the theater to start performing onstage. With my free hand (the other was rolling up a nylon) I began texting the stage manager to let her know I was running late. Before pressing "send" I felt my phone buzz.

It was my agent! What could she want late on a Friday night?

"Hi, Ann? I'm a little swamped. Can I call you back Monday?"

I had wedged my phone between my elbows because my left hand had gotten tangled in my bangs.

"Sorry, darling, can't do that. This is the big one. The prune in the pie. You hearing me, crackerjack?"

She cackled.

I was hearing her all right, but that wasn't the problem.

"Um, what exactly do you mean?"

"Keep your saddle on."

"Okay."

In addition to sounding exactly like a Southern Carol Channing, Ann my agent made up phrases on the spot. I called it "Annglish." It was pretty charming, except for the fact that I couldn't understand what she was saying.

"You've got an audition. For *Wicked*."

I nearly dropped the phone.

"*What?*"

"You got cotton in your ears? *Wicked*. Elphaba cover. San Francisco."

"No, no, I heard you. That's fantastic! When is it?"

"This Monday. Not busy this weekend, are you?"

I had three *Hee-Haw* performances over the next two days, then weekday rehearsals for a strange and inexplicable Chanukah musical I'd agreed to perform in the following weekend. Plus, my family would be in town.

"Uh, nope."

"Good! Practice, practice, practice."

"I will."

"You take your aim before you shoot, 'cause a shot like this hardly ever comes around."

"Right. Definitely."

"I'll send details. Cancel all your plans."

She hung up as my cab arrived at the theater. With no time to understand what had happened, I pegged my driver with a wad of cash, gathered my plastic bag-totes, and hobbled in stilettos over a snow bank into the theater's back entrance.

At 7:55 p.m. I exploded through the doors to find a deserted dressing room, except for my stage manager, who was there flapping her arms and jumping up and down either in silent panic or because she was playing a one-person game of charades in which the answer was "murder Felicia." Without pause I began buttoning up my corset, drenching my hair in Aqua Net, guzzling a water bottle, and smearing on lipstick, all while honking out a vocal warm-up that sounded exactly like a car alarm. After a brief mirror consultation I realized that one of my fake eyelashes had nestled over my top lip like a Hitler mustache. I ripped it off, which was kind of like an upper-lip wax.

I sprinted to my pre-show post, where I joined the rest of the cast just in time for the "places" call. Having crossed the finish line, I celebrated a breathless victory, trying to mutter "booyah" through my panting, but being too out of breath to mutter anything, then considering briefly how the only thing lamer than actually saying "booyah" was *trying* to say "booyah," but failing.

Still, I had made it, against all odds. For now I was out on top, teeming with confidence, like I could do anything—maybe, I thought, even nail my audition for *Wicked*.

Ah, the feeling of triumph!

I'd gotten a life-changing call that night. And I was ready to take on the world! Sweet victory would be mine.

Then I walked onstage without a skirt.

❖   ❖   ❖

"The wizard..."

—in a maneuver I'd learned days before, I sucked in my butt cheeks—

"aaaaaaand I!"

—and held out the final note for as long as I could. Meanwhile my hands floated up from my sides and over my head, as if I was launching into flight. As the final stream of air escaped me, I felt like I might next wilt to the floor, a balloon that had rapidly deflated.

My eyes refocused to the room. I looked at Craig, who was smiling.

That wasn't so bad, was it? I felt kind of giddy, either because I'd done well or because not enough oxygen was flowing to my brain.

"That was great," he said. "Now let's do the Cub Scene."

I had stayed up late memorizing my Elphaba lines, but decided to duck over to the piano to retrieve my script. An actor friend once told me that holding the script at an audition gave you an advantage; it was a kind of visual reminder that your performance was still unpolished, so the casting folks would be more forgiving.

Papers in hand, I retook my post in the center of the room. Faux Hawk had perked up and was reaching for some pages on the table, which meant he was probably my reader.

"Readers" are usually professional actors hired to play scene partner to every person who rolls through an audition. But in preliminary rounds, like this one, the reader is often the casting director himself, or his casting assistant.

"Whenever you're ready," said Craig.

I glanced at Faux Hawk, whose eyes narrowed. Through the silence I could almost feel my hand twitching, eager to spray him with little finger gun bullets.

The scene began. Faux Hawk spoke in a Keanu Reeves monotone. But this wasn't so bad. You might even say his standoffishness served his character—Fiyero, the self-absorbed playboy, *Wicked*'s male romantic lead.

As the scene drew to a close, Craig looked pleased.

"Great," he said. "How about some 'Defying Gravity?'"

Gulp.

How about it?

❖ ❖ ❖

As luck would have it, I happened to know a girl who'd played Elphaba before. Her name was Julie and she'd performed a bunch of times as the Broadway standby. The month before my audition we acted together in a workshop, and in our free time had chatted about bowling parties and affordable hair highlighting. Naturally, we were close Facebook friends. I contacted her the evening after my skirt-less *Hee-Haw* turn, and she graciously agreed to coach me.

We met at a (moderately jail-esque) midtown studio and dove headfirst into the audition material. There, listening intently, it took me all of three minutes to realize that I was completely and utterly screwed.

It was just—well? I'd had a hunch the Elphaba material would be hard to sing. But I'd never expected it to be impossible.

How can I explain this?

The songs were *high*. As in, the freaking notes were really, really freaking *high*. The audition material was a sinister collection of the hardest, highest, and most intense sections. They were also relentless—with no chance to regroup, and no room to fudge the interpretation so that, say, Elphaba whispers because she's lovelorn or hiding from the secret police. Nope, these songs were power anthems, emphatic cries sung during the absolute height of passion.

It was go big—or go home!

In light of this, the audition felt less like a lucky break and more like Luck had just whooped me on the ass with a horseshoe—as if to say,

"Here's your chance. Now fail!"

But Julie assured me I shouldn't panic; the songs were sing-able. Without missing a beat, she opened her mouth to demonstrate, and I nearly imploded. Her singing was so effortless it made me doubt she was a real person and not some extremely convincing human-shaped synthesizer. I gave her the once-over. Blonde-haired, blue-eyed, attractive. Was she, like all other Elphabas, scientifically engineered?

"Okay, your turn."

My pulse started to race.

What gives?

It wasn't even the audition yet.

Truth is, I'd always been insecure about my singing. Not having gone to college for theater, I'd dabbled in voice lessons, but never trained intensively. Sure, I knew about breathing from your diaphragm and all that, but learned to sing mostly by a method I liked to call "Guess and Check"—guess a way to sing something, check to see if it sounds good. If so, great. If not? Adjust.

Would my do-it-yourself approach fly in the face of the impossible?

Julie was peering at me with searching eyes, like a stern-browed headmistress. I counted off in my head, planted my feet, and started singing a few bars of the Act I Finale, "Defying Gravity." I managed to hang in until the end, but soon it got way too high and relentless, and I had to stop.

"Um, yeah—great!" Julie said.

I would have maybe half-believed her if my throat didn't feel like it had just been slathered in razor butter.

Julie said she'd observed a few imbalances in my posture, which may have been compromising my singing support. My left knee had a habit of bending inward and collapsing my hips, she said, which threw off my diaphragm and short-changed my breathing.

"To fix this," she advised, "tighten your butt, really hard."

She demonstrated, and I stared, enthralled. And not just because she had a totally rockin' butt.

Who knew it all came down to butt clenching?

I could definitely do this; I'd been clenching my butt for years! Just ask anyone who's ever known me at an academic institution.

We worked a bit more, the goal being for me to align my body and suck in my glutes with a vengeance. I next applied these principles to "The Wizard and I," whose excerpt was twice as long, though slightly less terrifying than "Defying Gravity." One of the tricks here was to adjust the vowels of the lyrics sung on super high notes. For example, final lyrics, "the Wizard and I," were actually sung as, "the Wizard aaaa naaaa." (Like you were saying the middle vowel of "banana.") The listener's ear, Julie explained, would be tricked into thinking they'd heard it right. Same went for "Defying Gravity." At the end of the song the lyrics were "bring me down." But I would actually sing, "bring maaaa naaaa."

What is this crazy singer voodoo, I thought as I clenched my butt once more, gearing up to sing. In a leap of faith, I tried it.

"The Wizard....aaaa naaaa!"

In the end, Julie promised that no matter my difficulties now, I would eventually be able to sing Elphaba. I just needed to practice every day.

This was great news, except for the fact that the audition was in less than forty-eight hours. Would I pull through, I wondered, given the time constraints?

Next, we read the confrontation scene between Elphaba and Glinda, *Wicked*'s other main character. "Don't be afraid to really let her have it," Julie told me after one run-through. "Elphaba doesn't take crap from anybody. She's brave, and sticks her neck out."

I flashed back to the time I had seen *Wicked* on Broadway five years before, when I couldn't help but feel a strong connection to the character. Elphaba was fiery, like me, but also sensitive, bookish, and awkward, with a confused fashion sense. (Like me.) Through outward greenness and inner strength, she was one-of-a-kind: a girl who would face, head-on, any challenge cast before her.

(My only wish? That Elphaba could audition in my place.)

"You know," Julie said, "once you've got the acting down, you'll find that singing the role is as much about emotion as it is about vocal technique. You have to reach inside yourself to find the source of what's causing Elphaba to sing so passionately. Practice good form, of course—but once you have that down, just let everything go."

Our session came to a close, and we hugged goodbye.

Alone in the studio, it was time to keep pounding the pavement. I'd typed up the lyrics to "Defying Gravity" on a separate sheet of paper, which helped me to visualize the lyrics as a story, as opposed to spread out across a musical score. As Julie had said, I needed to find the source of Elphaba's passion—to tap into something that meant something to me. To remember something that would resonate, emotionally.

❖   ❖   ❖

Two days later, nearing the end of my audition, I'd made it to the end of "Defying Gravity." I lowered my voice and rumbled from my gut, daring anyone who'd ever hurt me to try and do it again.

"Maaaa naaaa!"

I let go, releasing all of my sound, from head to toe.

Then it was over.

"Thank you, Felicia."

I looked over to the pianist then back to Craig, sweaty, out of breath. My mind was contracting, then expanding, and my body felt wrecked. I wandered over to the piano to get my stuff, then back to the door.

"Thanks."

As I turned the knob, tears started to run down my cheeks. I didn't know the exact reason, but my body was telling me it was time to cry.

Back in the terminal, I reunited with Lipstick Loop and the other misfit toys. Teardrops speckled my burgundy collar, which fed down toward my armpit stains, like two rivers meeting the sea. I imagined I must have looked exactly as the others had: bleary-eyed, dazed, a shell of a person.

"Fierce," I heard somebody say.

"Fierce!"

After changing into jeans in a bathroom stall (pleasantly larger than a dog kennel), I consulted the mirror. My nose had become positively clown-like from crying, and the only course of action was to deploy urgent de-puffing reinforcements. As I blotted it with a cold paper towel, it occurred to me that if I ever had to cry on camera, they would need a wide-angle HD lens to capture the girth and saturation of my truly majestic schnozzer.

Once my nose was no longer visible from space, I took the elevator down to street level, since it was time to head to my afternoon Chanukah rehearsal. As I walked through the glass double-doors, I caught sight of a familiar silhouette hovering on the sidewalk. He turned and smiled, scooping me up for a bear hug.

"Marshall! What the—!"

Enter Marshall Evan Roy, my brand new sort-of boyfriend of several weeks. He was caring, reliable, told me how he felt, loved to cook, and had the physique of a Greek god. With a man that perfect, there had to be drawbacks. I was certain that one of these days I would see his face plastered on the news, below the headline, "Con Artist Slash Occasional Fitness Model Dupes Heartbreak-Weary Girl Into Thinking He's Perfect, Steals Her Bananas."

It would be a long headline. But, still: it was such an obvious plot twist.

"You mentioned the name of the casting office over the phone," Marshall said, "so I Googled it. I wanted to surprise you. Here." He handed me a baggy. "I brought you an oatmeal raisin cookie."

"Marshall! How the—!"

I was speaking in half-phrases, a dead giveaway that the cat had gotten my tongue and the butterflies had colonized my stomach. "Thank you," I said, through a mouthful of oatmeal and raisins, planting an ill-timed cookie-crumb kiss on Marshall's lips.

He had shown up unannounced, but Marshall's thoughtfulness came as no surprise. Instead, it was a trend; from gourmet dinners, to homemade cocktails, to tickets to Broadway shows, our dates so far had been off-the-charts.

(**GREEN.** 5. fresh, recent, or new: *a green relationship*)

We'd been set up on a blind group date by mutual friends from childhood, his best friend Francesca and my best friend Becky, who, for years, had been pitching me like the next billion-dollar ad campaign. Our date location of choice was (brace yourself) Serendipity on the Upper East Side—the one from that terrible John Cusack movie. (*"You don't have to understand. You just have to have faith!" "Faith in what?" "Destiny!"*)

On said group date, at one point I squeezed Marshall's upper arm. Based on what I felt, he earned a second, solo date. I do not remember any of this second date, so distracted was I by the fact that I was out with someone, (1) who looked like a gladiator, (2) who wasn't brain-dead or sociopathic, (3) whose company I was starting to really enjoy. What I *do* remember is I was served one whole sea bass, with eye and bones intact, on a wooden slab. Rather than send it back, I chewed down the fish, bones and all, as if this were my regular practice, which was an early sign that I was falling for him.

A few dates more and I accepted an after-dinner invitation to have tea at his place.

You heard me: *tea!* Because "tea" is code for "I spent the night." Chastely!

(Okay, not in the true Catholic sense of the word. But we *were* able to resist our lightning-bolt mutual attraction, i.e. nobody scored a homerun, i.e. do you want me to spell it out for you? i.e. we didn't have sex, i.e. but we made out.)

The next morning I woke to homemade eggs and toast, my impossibly muscular chef decked out in nothing but boxer briefs and a striped scarf, which I first observed through the frame of his kitchen doorway, squinting my eyes so it resembled the watercolor book jacket of a romance novel. (I can see it now, in paperback: *The Brooklyn Scoundrel: Omelets of Sin.*)

I slinked over to the kitchen table, where I commented on the fact that Marshall was left-handed.

"Just like Obama."

"Or Sarah Jessica Parker," he said.

We lazed into the afternoon, eating eggs with globs of goat cheese, bantering ten miles a minute, at which point I realized that not only was this guy a total hunk, but he was—gasp!— smart, funny, and interesting.

Was dating supposed to be this great? History, political scandals, and all my prior boyfriends had taught me, no.

That day after my audition Marshall wore the same structured, burnt-brown leather jacket and plain white t-shirt he wore on our first date, which made him look a bit like James Dean (if James Dean were a giant, stylish gladiator). His hair had been mussed from the wind and hung in his eyes, in an unnerving "come hither" way—which made me want to obey, immediately, rubbing oatmeal cookie all over him, like some weird baker's porn.

"How did the audition go?" Marshall asked, putting his arms around my waist.

I chewed and swallowed.

"Oh, pretty okay," I said, telling him about Lipstick Loop, Faux Hawk, my unfortunate Western-themed introduction. In recounting it struck me: the audition hadn't been half bad.

"I'm sure you were awesome. Can I walk you to rehearsal?"

I did that *Seinfeld* thing where Elaine shoves Jerry.

"You remembered my skedge? What the—!"

Marshall grinned, his dimples revealing themselves, like commas in the run-on sentence of his cuteness.

"I'm always looking for excuses to see you," he said.

What was he selling! I mean, c'mon.

To better understand my skepticism about the entire male race, perhaps we should pause here and take a quick stroll through my Dating History Museum.

This vast, temperature-controlled space, curated by yours truly, houses tributes to the long lineage of questionable men to whom I've offered my pulsing, wound-weary heart.

Please place your umbrella in the bin, help yourself to an information pamphlet, and follow me inside (donation optional).

Beginning in the foyer, you'll see our Early Years Collection, when dysfunction first reared its head. As these posters and magazine cutouts reveal (fashioned to replicate my childhood bedroom), during my youth I retreated into elaborate fantasy worlds of celebrity romance. At five, I wrote Hulk Hogan a love letter (yes, the wrestler). At eight, I went steady with John Travolta (his chin butt made me swoon). At twelve, I was torn between Leonardo DiCaprio and Johnny Rzeznik from the Goo Goo Dolls (who could resist such messy coifs?). Later I had a mind fling with Richard Chamberlain (who didn't look a day older than 65), before becoming obsessed with Alan Cumming and the lead singer of *The Darkness* (Picasso had a Blue Period; I had an Androgynous Men Period). Most enduring was personal favorite Douglas Sills, star of Broadway's *The Scarlet Pimpernel*, whom I stalked outside the Minskoff Theater stage door on many occasions, aided and abetted by my musical theater-loving father.

As you'll note in the information pamphlet, through each torrid, make-believe affair, I mastered the art of projecting wonderful qualities onto men who did nothing at all to deserve it—which is pretty harmless in fantasy.

In real life, it can get dicey.

Wrapping around to the High School Collection, you'll see that my foray into the dating world proved less than ideal. Take a moment to examine the following busts: the Devout Jewish Kid Who Swore Off Shiksas After Me, the Possibly Bisexual Buddhist Whose Catch Phrase Was "Bros Before Hos," the Aspiring White Rapper Who Made Me His Secret Girlfriend, and, around the corner, a sculpture series I like to call the Four Gays. (As the information pamphlet confirms, yes, I did have four gay boyfriends.)

Finishing our tour, I invite you to the College Wing of the Museum, where I present another sculpture series known as the Three Matts, which represent the time in college when I dated three men named Matt consecutively. First we have Matt 1.0, who has earned a figurine, as opposed to a commemorative bust, since ours was a brief fling. He orchestrated my very first college hookup, a make-out session that began while we were studying Italian verbs.

("I'm not going to tell you the correct past participle," Matt 1.0 said, "unless you kiss me.")

Next you'll see a bust of Matt 2.0, the small bespectacled individual I dated on and off for two years. (You might remember him from our first scene, seeing *Wicked* on Broadway with my family.) As the pamphlet describes, our time together was pretty bizarre. On our first Valentine's Day Matt 2.0 took three drunk photos of me, made posters of them, and labeled them *Paradiso*, *Purgatorio*, and *Inferno*. Instead of going on dates we played Subjective Guess Who, a board game we invented that was exactly like Guess Who except you asked questions like, "Is your person a Democrat?" or, "Does your person recycle?" Appealing to each other's totally weird sides was fun for a while, but not sustainable. In our case, I cut things off with Matt 2.0 just in time for Matt 3.0.

You'll find him all the way across the room.

As the ex-boyfriend responsible for my greatest heartbreak, Matt 3.0 has earned not a bust but a mini mausoleum, engraved with year and title (Breaker of Fel's Heart, 2006-2009). We dated through my junior and senior years then tentatively broke up, got back together, broke up, and got back together while he spent a year abroad in Paris.

Together we were destroying each other in the service of making things work. Because, you see, I had thought Matt 3.0 to be The One. You know, the person with whom I would spend the rest of my life, have babies, yada yada, blah blah.

(And as you'll note, the Museum room reserved for The One remains conspicuously empty.)

Why was I so foolish? Maybe it had something to do with end-of-college timing, or the fact that Matt 3.0 spun a fine "I love you forever and ever" yarn, or the fact that, in my Early Years, I'd been great at fabricating relationships.

But 56 tear-filled phone calls, 27 pints of Ben and Jerry's Chocolate Fudge Brownie, four and a half years, and three long, drawn-out breakups after I met Matt 3.0, I had a bracing reality check.

LL101: **Love hurts**.

I'd endured disappointments, rejections, and resentments, but I'd never *really* been hurt. No, not in a lasting way. Stunned into solitude, I vowed never to let it happen again.

So, given this tour of my dating history, I hope you can understand why I was reluctant to fall for this Marshall Roy character. This too-good-to-be-true, cookie-wielding hunk of a man.

But here I was, on a street corner in Manhattan, munching oatmeal and raisins, fawning over somebody who could very easily, with one swift chop, cleave my heart in two.

"Is it okay you're not at work?" I asked.

Marshall made a *pshaw* noise and batted an imaginary fly.

"I just told them I had to run an important errand. Which is true: it's important that I get a recap and give you a cookie."

"Well, then, lead the way," I said, doing an about-face toward the intersection.

We crossed the street together and began walking up 8th Avenue, holding hands through the cold.

3. GROUNDHOG DAY

Wicked's casting process is kind of like rolling admissions to a university—if that university accepted only one student, and didn't tell most applicants whether or not they got in. You "apply" on no real schedule, just whenever they happen to be casting, and hear back at any point in the future.

Or never.

Example: A friend of mine auditioned for *Wicked* many times, but it was almost a year before she finally heard that she'd landed the part of Glinda on the national tour. Another friend was offered the supporting role of Boq, the overlooked munchkin, but *Wicked* couldn't yet tell him where, or when, he would be needed. That's the university being like, "We want you at our school, we know what your major is going to be, but we don't know your campus or the year you'll graduate."

The week after my audition I practically chained myself to my phone, and not just because Marshall and I were texting about 1,000 times a day.

I was waiting. For it. You know!

The call.

In the meantime, I was rehearsing for my strange and inexplicable Chanukah musical which, despite being mind-numbing, at least gave me something to keep me occupied. The days crawled by until it was Friday—weekend two of *Hee-Haw* performances. Another distraction from the waiting.

The old "don't call us, we'll call you" Hollywood cliché is more or less true of New York theater, although I've never heard anybody actually say it while smoking a cigar or slamming a door in my face. But the sentiment is alive and well. As an actor, you have to be ready for everything—and nothing. After an audition, there's no promise of hearing back, of getting feedback, or of finding closure. And this is absolutely true of *Wicked*—it being such a massive, multi-pronged operation, with productions running all over the world. They're busy, and they have a lot going on. You're spending your days pretending to be a babushka bubbe making latkes and applesauce. They're thousands strong, with millions of fans.

You're one person, and you live alone.

See the difference?

On Friday, Marshall and I rendezvoused an hour before my *Hee-Haw* call time. I spotted a small café near the theater and proposed we duck in for tea and cake, mostly because this required that Marshall carry me over a huge pile of snow. As we ordered a plate of sweets, the cashier told us, in a French accent, that she saw Marshall's snow-bank heroics and found us romantic. It reminded her, she said, of the couple seated by the window, a pair of regulars who were celebrating their fifty-year anniversary.

"How wonderful, at once, to see the bud of love and love in full bloom."

It was so sweet, I almost vomited. French café? A prediction of lifelong love? The cliché gods were smiling down on us—just as they had for weeks, ever since our *serendipitous* (groan) meeting.

Only now—as the weirdly prophetic French lady had reminded us—we were inching closer to that scary L-word.

You know. The one that rhymes with "shove"—and is equally jarring.

We seated ourselves in front of a window, across from the fifty-year couple, at which point Marshall made quick work of a massive mound of chocolate cake, while I stared at him, remembering the boxer-brief-striped-scarf-omelet incident.

"Hey," I said, "I like you."

"I like you, too," he said, his mouth smeared with chocolate.

"If I don't get *Wicked*, it won't be so bad," I said. I didn't know what possessed me.

"But you're going to get it," said Marshall.

"Nah. I think I would have heard by now."

I scooped up a lemon square and began chomping, upholding the tradition that our every exchange should involve mouthfuls of saturated fats and/or sugary carbohydrates.

Then, as if sensing I wasn't on my guard, the phone rang.

❖   ❖   ❖

Callbacks are the ultimate déjà vu experience, but without any humor or Bill Murray charm.

My Monday *Wicked* callback began exactly like the prior week's audition, with only minor revisions: shower warm-up, with different, less exfoliating body wash, followed by ritual banana consumption, followed by the donning of an outfit that was distinctly not burgundy satin, but cotton and black (a pit-stain shield!).

Soon I was back in the neon airport terminal. No Lipstick Loop, no fierce bald men, only a bunch of new girls eyeing each other. I wondered how many there were of them, total. Not just in the room, but in the world, going about their days, stacking the odds against me.

The extent of my guppyhood in an expanding sea of fish suddenly hit me.

Still, I'd do my best. If likelihood of getting cast was proportional to time and effort spent preparing, honestly? Maybe I did have a shot in hell. I'd worked and worked and worked some more. If I didn't get it, it wouldn't be for lack of trying.

Soon Craig appeared, leading me back to the same room as before, where this time there was no Faux Hawk (and no finger guns). In his place were a bunch of new faces: a tiny girl wearing roman sandals, even though it was winter; a man behind the piano with wet curls, named either Lombardo or Dominick; a man with a shaved head and piercing blue eyes, named Paul, Alan, or Nick (I have a strange deficit for recalling names; it's one of two reasons I could never be in politics—the other is I hate wearing pantsuits).

"Okay, 'Wizard and I,' whenever you're ready."

The callback packet was the exact same material as the audition, so, amidst the weekend circus of wild commutes to *Hee-Haw* in dressing rooms that move, I had spent my time building on what I'd already learned with Julie—improving, enhancing, and stepping up my Elphaba game.

The main goal? Just stay focused.

Runners, on your marks!

The vamp of rolling chords began, and soon I was off to a sprint. And just when it felt like my shoelaces might come undone, the finish-line ribbon split across my body.

"Very nice," said Paul-Alan-Nick.

"Could you wait outside for a sec?" said Craig.

I walked into the waiting room. From all the sweating it felt like I'd given myself a shower, and my body turned frigid. Once seated, I wedged my ice-cold hands under my thighs. Somehow both ablaze with heat and trembling from cold, as I waited for Craig to reappear I felt like I'd been caught beneath the top layer of a frozen lake, where the water below had begun to boil.

The door swung open and I saw Craig approaching, the camera frame of my view zooming in on his tired face, his eyes crinkling up into what could be a smile or the expression of someone who would have to let me down.

"Felicia, can you come to a dance call at 3:45 today?"

"Um, yes."

Back in my studio apartment I rooted through nests of dirty clothing, dry-cleaning hangers, electric wires, and power strips.

Where are my dance clothes?

I'm not really a dancer, and I hate anything that is tight and clingy. But my hope was that some forgotten spandex relic would materialize from the ashes—a haggard, molting phoenix, leftover from my days of high school recitals.

I looked around my apartment.

What a crap hole.

I'd been spending so much time with Marshall—whipping in and out after work, preparing for auditions, or late date nights, trying to give myself salon blowouts—over the past several weeks I'd embraced being an absolute slob. Things never plunged to health-hazard depths, but it wasn't unusual for me to wake up in the morning to find my entire library of books and Xeroxed sheet music either on my lap or directly under my head, with my computer propped up on socks and books, playing *This American Life* episodes on repeat.

Finally, I came upon a probably clean pair of American Apparel biker shorts, which were bright red with white piping, and barely grazed the top of my thigh. They reminded me of an adult diaper, if adult diapers were made of retro-colored cotton. I also managed to excavate a navy tank top and a pair of navy leggings. Everything combined made me look like a patriotic diaper-wearing sailor who had shrunk his uniform in the wash. At the last minute I decided to throw on yet another shirt, an homage to the 80s that was peach pink and fell off of my shoulders.

My theory? The more clothes I wore, the less likely anyone would be able to see my pit stains with the naked eye. (Downside: more layers would actually make me sweat *more*. But that was my silent cross to bear.)

I wolfed down another good-luck banana, threw on a pair of running sneakers, and dashed out the door.

The callback studio was in a different building in midtown. I took an elevator to a long hallway on the umpteenth floor, with huge numbered doors. I made my way down to the far right, opened the door, and saw a small waiting area with a leather couch and stools, on which there were two girls and two boys, each looking down at their cell phones.

"Is this the *Wicked* dance callback?" I said to the air.

One of the boys looked up.

"You got it!"

He was very chipper.

One girl had curly brown hair and was about my type, while the other was tiny-boned and olive-skinned, with sunken cheeks and pin-straight black hair. Kind of like a figure in an Edvard Munch painting, except pretty.

No one was talking, so, given the tension, it was obviously my duty to flout social norms.

"So, are you ladies going to wear character shoes or sneakers?" I said, theatrically rooting through my bag, as if I even had a choice.

"Sneakers, probably," the brunette said.

"Yeah, sneakers," said Edvard Munch.

"Oh, cool." I turned to the boys. "What part are you here for?"

"Fiyero cover. It's for immediate casting on Tour One. We would leave on Monday. Can you even believe it?"

The two boys looked so alike it was hard to tell which one was talking.

"Wow! That's crazy."

"I know."

"And it's just you two guys?"

"So it seems!" said one boy to the other. Or maybe they were speaking in unison?

I could only assume the two girls were going in for my part—ensemble/Elphaba understudy. But I was too scared to ask.

Sunlight streamed through the windows, a taunting contrast to the thick cloud of tension that hung over us all. Something about it being a small group raised the stakes, and made me want to start slapping everybody. If I'd had a choice, I would have preferred a huge "cattle call" audition. Not only would the competition be faceless, nameless, and less intimidating, but when we got into the studio I could disappear behind a cluster of *real* dancers and, if necessary, duck out the fire escape. At least then I could save face, bowing out of this dreamlike experience with a pathetic whimper, not a humiliating bang.

However you slice them, dance auditions suck—especially for hacks like me. Sure, I'd had years of dance training growing up—and, accordingly, traumatic John Travolta anecdotes from year-end recitals—but in the triple-threat zone of singer-actor-dancer, I knew the last one fell lowest on my résumé of theater skills. If given enough time, I could pick up most dance combinations, as long as they didn't require exceptional technique or that I touch my toes.

But in a fast-paced audition? I knew I was toast.

All of a sudden a side door swung open, and in drifted a woman with burgundy hair and low-slung dancer pants.

"Come in," she said.

We were told, (1) that this woman's name was either Corinne or something else, (2) that we would learn a combination that pieced together the hardest ensemble dancing from the show, and (3) that our audition would, for whatever reason, be accompanied by live drumming.

Actually, we weren't told that last part, but it was probable from the fact that there was a man sitting on a stool behind a drum set. Maybe he would provide snare, high-hat drum kicks every time I would make a joke, and by "make a joke" I mean try to dance. Whatever the case, the drums felt extravagant—like the callback mattered all the more. Which made me feel all the worse.

"Okay," said Corinne, "Let's start with the 'Hoi Polloi.'"

This sounded like a Vietnamese sandwich, but was actually a dance routine involving much stepping, pivoting, changing of direction, and general chaos. The main challenge, it seemed, was not only to remember which foot to walk on when, and in which direction, but to do so while looking like you had no joints.

As soon as the music started I jolted forward and slammed into Edvard Munch and then a table.

"I'm not so much concerned with your getting the steps right," Corinne said to us as the wall and I met. "I want to see that *pop, pow!* I want to see you *hitting it.*"

As she said this she threw her body forward with full force then stopped her momentum by going completely rigid. She did this a few more times, apparently to demonstrate some choreographic sequence, but I saw no pattern whatsoever; just an endless cycle of stopping and starting, each time with board-straight limbs, as you might do when you are nervously, and indecisively, fleeing the scene of your own crime.

"Okay, let me see you guys *give it to me.*"

The drums cut in, as if to startle us into dance, and it kind of worked. My lower body moved in whatever direction it wanted, aimlessly walking back and forth, while my upper body essentially just did The Robot.

It was obvious the guys were way better than we of the fairer sex. Even though the two girls *looked* more like dancers than I did—which is to say, their outfits didn't resemble an incontinent sailor's—I was pleased to see that we were in the same boat: discombobulated and miserable. In between each pass at the routine together we cowered in the corner, where we were on the one hand united by suffering, and on the other hand fighting off a *Lord of the Flies* instinct—poised for strangling, punching, gouging, hair ripping. You know: your usually audition-y stuff.

After about 20 minutes the door opened and Craig the casting director entered, his collar popped, his head hanging down to consult his smartphone.

This was the worst thing that could happen, in my opinion, as I was at that moment bright red, my hair so drenched it looked like I had just gone swimming. I glanced around. Everyone else was dry and Edvard Munch's hair was miraculously kempt.

"Okay, are you ready to break off into groups? Let's see guys, then girls. C'mon, *give it to me.*"

Drum fill, followed by a blast of music. The guys took off, prancing around like the best of them, hitting each step with ease and agility.

"Girls, let's do it up. Make it count and *work it.*"

This was the inevitable moment of judgment, when we had to "perform for real." Whereas before it was somehow not the actual audition, now it "counted," which is ridiculous-sounding, I know, but that's how dance auditions go.

The music kept vamping, drums keeping a steady beat, until we were off.

As I propelled forward, I kept my knees locked while standing on my tiptoes, swiveling around, shooting out one foot forward, then the next. I basically just flailed, hoping my willingness to injure myself would count for something.

I mean, look at me!

I was the most insane robot dancer you'd ever *seen*, whipping and prancing around like it was my last dying wish to convulse to live drums.

When it was over I found myself in the corner of the room opposite from everyone else. The other girls, also scattered about, seemed just as confused.

This was great news. There's nothing like the thrill of realizing your competition isn't so bad after all—or, I should say, *is* bad. It's a terrible, sick feeling of evil pleasure. But, if you've ever auditioned for anything, you know what I'm talking about.

I traipsed to the other side of the room, poised to grab my water bottle and head out the door. But the torture had only just begun.

We had to learn *another* combination, a hybrid of random steps from a bunch of songs throughout the show tacked onto something called the "Ozdust Ballroom" dance. In this combination, we had to spin ourselves in various directions, while tangling and coiling our hands around our wrists, squatting, jumping, and hitting various "broken scarecrow," positions, which for me meant I, again, did The Robot, while spazzing out.

As we danced I eyed Craig, lurking by the door, beside the drummer, texting. I could only imagine he was corresponding with some *Wicked* higher up, writing something to the effect of:

Craig: 4:14PM no castable girls. may have to cancel everything.

Snare, high-hat drum kick! And here we go!

I spun around, flopped down, then shot up off the ground, my arms and legs kicking and bucking in many directions, as I imagined someone would do if they got pricked while going to the bathroom, bare-assed, in the woods.

What now?

My right brain swung into gear, and all of a sudden I was repeating the first part of the dance—the little bit I happened to remember—once, twice, three times.

John Travolta, here I come.

I flicked and kicked around with the *pop, pow!* Corinne was referring to earlier. After all, it wasn't about the steps, right? Maybe it *was* just about showing her my potential—even if learning the steps might not happen until some rare, distant, apocalyptic day.

The drums came to an abrupt halt. In my periphery I saw Edvard Munch still spinning, caught in her own momentum, until she eventually wound down to stillness.

Corinne sat in a wide dancer split at the front of the room, looking distraught, her head cradled in her hands.

"Okay, why don't you all hang outside for a bit," she said.

Back in the hallway the vibe was tenser than ever, and instead of trying to talk I simply buckled under the pressure, curling up on the couch in the fetal position.

"So have you guys been in for *Wicked* before?" asked one of the boy-twins.

"Never."

"Nope."

"Nah," I chimed in.

"I was seen a while back," said the other boy-twin. "For Fiyero cover in another company. So I know the dances pretty well."

Just as I was about to start sucking my thumb, the studio door opened and Corinne and Craig reappeared. They were both smiling like pageant contestants.

"Thanks so much, guys, for all of your hard work today. Everybody can leave."

Yep. There it was.

We're toast.

"Except Felicia—could you please stay behind a minute?"

I sort of did a spit-take, but without any liquid in my mouth, which meant I basically made a fart noise with my lips.

"Sure thing!" I said, jerking my body upright.

"Come on into the studio."

As I re-laced my sneakers, the others milled through the exit, silent and gazing at the floor. I felt a twinge of survivor's guilt. If the tables were turned, I knew I'd be crushed. Or worse, totally pissed, ready to go Jerry Springer on their asses.

Whatever the case, I had to keep it together: this could be my chance to actually succeed in fooling *Wicked* into casting me! I shook myself awake and stepped inside the studio.

"We're going to teach you some lifts," said Corinne. "Do you have any experience doing lifts?"

"Not really. But I have been known to lift things," I said.

"We need to see you do the lifts that would be part of your ensemble track," Corinne said.

"Right," I said.

"This is Patrick," she continued, as a strapping man in a tank top emerged from nowhere and stood before me. "He'll be lifting you."

"Hello."

"Okay, for the first lift I need you to bend your knees, lift off with Patrick, come to a *passé* in the air, extend your hand like this, and then come down to bent knees on the dismount."

She demonstrated.

"Do you think you can do this?"

"Definitely," I lied.

"Okay, let's give it a try."

I nudged my way into Patrick's arms where we fidgeted to establish a grip on my waist.

"It's okay," he said. "I got you. Let's try lifting off. Aaaaand, *bend your knees!*"

I obeyed, and, without warning, I was springing up into the air, where I was instantly afraid for my life. If Patrick lifted Corinne like a snack pack of air-popped chips, I was swinging around like a sack of overgrown potatoes.

"Oh, dear *God!*" I cried.

Worried that Patrick would not be able to support my weight, I reached for his body with my legs and tried to wrap them around his torso for stability. Not only did this not help matters, but, while being lowered, my foot slid down his abdomen and plunged directly onto his crotch. I turned and saw his face was bright red and contorted.

"I am so sorry," I said, meaning it.

"I don't even know what you're talking about," he replied.

"Not bad," said Corinne, clearly lying. "Let's try it again."

So we did. Similar deal this time: instant terror, followed by spastic body flailing, followed by ungraceful contact with any number of inappropriate regions on Patrick's body, followed by my feeling like a complete buffoon.

"Okay, let's do it again," said Corinne.

After about nine passes, everyone agreed in unspoken terms that we'd had enough of wagering Patrick's manhood, and so we moved on.

To another freakin' lift.

"Here I want you to focus on the back-bending, on really collapsing backwards over his shoulder," Corinne said as she is hoisted over a twirling Patrick, to hang there, limply, yet somehow elegantly, like a self-possessed ragdoll.

"Do you think you can do that?" she called out to me, hanging upside down.

Nope.

"Uh huh."

As I flopped down over Patrick, my torso felt like it had been turned inside out. While I tried to recreate that same sense of release I saw in Corinne, my legs jutted out at a 90-degree angle, spinning like the blade-teeth of a whirling hacksaw, until I almost sliced through Corinne's lithe frame.

In a fit of embarrassment, I let out a horrible giggle as I was lowered onto the floor.

"Wow, I did not know my legs would do that," I said, giggling, horribly.

"Again!" commanded Corinne, so we repeated the second lift, over and over.

It was impossible to say whether I was staying afloat or slowly sinking. Each time we practiced I searched Corinne and Patrick's faces for some sign of hope, some sign that I was still in the game.

Occasionally, they'd smile, as if it were only a matter of time before the good news would wash over me.

If I can just keep it together a little longer...

Or was it all a big, fat lie? Prolonging matters, getting my hopes up for the inevitable disappointment?

(**GREEN**. 3. Simple; unsophisticated; gullible; easily fooled: *a green newcomer.*)

That night I fell asleep to flashbacks of inverted, spinning rooms, the nightmarish memory of teetering over Patrick's shoulder, moments before I would crash to the ground.

As I drifted off to sleep, I wondered, over and over,

What happens now?

4. DON'T WORRY, YOU'LL FIT

The next day my stomach back-flipped every time the phone rang.

9:49 a.m. Wake-up call from a New York area code. Could this be it?

From the casting office? From Ann's home phone? From the Wizard of Oz himself?!

My prescription was ready at Walgreens.

10:25 a.m. Unknown number from a blocked caller!

Aaaand....it was my mother, over at my Grandma Yola's house, asking if I'd heard anything.

"Um, *no*, Mom," I groaned, "but thanks for the blocked-caller blue balls."

"The *what?*"

"Nevermind."

"What did she say," I heard Grandma Yola shouting in the background.

12:01 p.m. The phone rang while I was washing dishes in my sink. Caller ID said it was my agent.

Sweet Mother of God.

I dried my hands, and with trembling fingers opened my phone to choke out a greeting.

"Hello?"

"Good news!" Ann growled. "Good, good, good news," she said again. "Really good news."

"Ann! What's the good news?"

"You're *Wicked*'s first choice!"

I couldn't believe it, so I screamed.

"But, see now, here's the beef," said Ann. "They need you to go to a costume fitting to see if you can, well, fit into the costumes."

"Wait, what?"

"Before they cast you, they need to double check. I'd say there's a great chance you're gonna get it, darlin'."

"Okay, that is pretty great news!"

"But we can't count our hens."

"Right," I said, taking a gulp. "So, when is the costume fitting?"

"Today, in two hours. Does that work for you?"

Hmm. What was on my agenda for the day? (1) Fret, (2) Worry, (3) Mull, (4) Pace, (5) Relive every moment of callback to calculate hypothetical chances, (6) Pick up Walgreens prescription.

"I think I can make it."

"Perfect."

"But, Ann—what if I don't fit into the costumes?"

I glanced over at my full-length mirror, sucking in my cheeks and stomach, like a constipated fish, immediately regretting my unrestrained Italian feast of a Thanksgiving, as well as every single dessert-fueled date I'd had with Marshall.

"Don't worry," she said, "you'll fit."

I'd jotted down directions to the *Wicked* costume shop on a scrap of paper I found in my bed, and as I wound along the sidewalk in the Garment District I scoured the buildings for street numbers. This part of town was unfamiliar, and kind of deteriorating; a gentle throwback to the older New York I'd only seen in 1970s documentaries about drug lords and social justice. Finally I stumbled across what appeared to be the doorway in question, and so I ambled inside.

While nothing about it was fishy, the building felt almost like a secret hideout. Who would have suspected that *Wicked*—the worldwide mega-phenomenon—would have a modest costume shop chilling in some random, non-descript building? Okay, maybe anyone with deductive reasoning skills, but still. It felt like I was uncovering a mystery.

What will I discover?

The possibilities were endless. *Wicked*, for me, still existed on a magical otherworldly plane. The closer I came to peering at its reality, the more I felt myself becoming timid.

What's more, this day—these next few moments, even—could mark the end of my journey. It was possible that after getting fitted I'd come up short—or tall, or wide, or narrow, or any other less-than-ideal measurement.

I knocked on a large door, and a light-haired girl answered.

"Hello!" I bellowed. "I'm looking for Amanda?"

"Just one moment," the girl said, beckoning for me to come inside.

As I did, I was transported to another world.

Stacked from floor to ceiling were rows upon rows of glimmering shapes, colors, and layered fabric. The *Wicked* costumes shone in palettes of teal, deep greens, gold flourishes, couched in an exuberant tangle of curling, structured appendages—quirky embellishments that extended from the costumes like outstretched hands, inviting me to join this catalog of beauty. Dotting the wardrobe racks every few inches were people's names—presumably former cast members.

"Are you Felicia?"

A thin-faced woman walked toward me, holding out a sheet of paper.

"I am," I said, extending my hand for a shake.

"Amanda. I just need you to fill this out and we can get going."

The sheet in question was an inquisition of my basic measurements—height, weight, shoe size—which, of course, put me on the defensive.

"When you say 'weight,' do you mean weight with clothes on or off?"

"What?" said Amanda, as she reached for her measuring tape, pencil, and pins.

"Oh, nevermind," I recanted, debating in my head which number sounded more castable: an even 130 or a willy-nilly 134. I settled on 127. But I didn't stop there.

"So, um, my dress size is actually different for my shirt and pants, so it varies. Should I put both?"

"Sure."

"Now, when you say, 'shoe size' do you mean to say—"

"Here," Amanda said, cutting in, "for that I'm going to do a tracing of your foot."

She slapped a sheet of paper on the floor and started tracing, which was my cue to strike the least casual of casual conversations.

"So, have you, uh, like, seen anybody else today for measurements?"

Amanda wasn't fazed.

"People are in and out of the shop all the time. I wasn't here this morning, so I'm not sure."

"Oh, cool," I replied, biting my lip, rolling out my ankles to impress Amanda with my arches.

"So, are all of the costumes kept here?"

"Each production has its own wardrobe department, but yes, when the costumes aren't being used they're housed here. Our goal today is to find some that might fit you."

She led me to the right aisle and started hoisting down clusters of hangers, on which there had been draped every manner of heavy fabric, sewn together in intricate and impossible designs. These costumes were so large and elaborate that some looked more like wildly festive outdoor tents than any kind of wardrobe for humans. She held out my first costume, which reminded me of a brownish orange barrel held together by a structure of hoops, studs, and snaps.

Utterly perplexed, my first instinct was to initiate a headfirst attack—so I just basically lunged forward with my chin tucked to my chest, like a land diver. This was apparently very wrong.

"Oh, nope, careful there," said Amanda. "It looks like it buttons *here*, but actually you just pull it apart with the snaps *there*, and step inside right *there*."

She pried apart the barrel, then collapsed it around me, until I was swimming in hoops and fabric.

"Over time, you would learn how to get everything on and off, plus you'd have a dresser helping you during the actual show."

"This is great news because I can barely dress myself," I said.

We tried on several more costumes for my potential ensemble track, and each time I said a silent prayer that I'd be able to fit. By some miracle, nothing tore or burst, even when we layered one or more costumes on top of each other—a method that allowed for quick changes during the show.

So far, so good.

Next we made our way to a library of plastic bins containing dozens of colorful shoes. They were labeled in Sharpie with names of former *Wicked* cast members. It seemed the production kept a record of everyone who had ever passed through—a monument to the talent that had helped make it possible. I browsed names that read like chapter headings in a theater encyclopedia: Idina Menzel, Eden Espinosa, Shoshana Bean, Julia Murney, Ana Gasteyer. Confronted by this visual reminder of how small I was, I felt my throat *gulp*, in that cartoon sort of way.

"Hmm," said Amanda, kneading her palms together. "Why don't we give those a try—the Elphaba shoes."

She scooped up one of the bins and started to dig. I peered over her shoulder to see folds of supple leather, zippers, and lace, doubling back on each other, like some swirling shoe orgy, until a handsome pair of brown laced boots emerged from the chaos. They'd been fashioned to look worn and distressed, and so carried with them inalienable character and story, like an old medicine man.

"Here we go," Amanda said.

I took a deep breath and slinked my foot toward her, as if the boot had to first grant me permission to enter its domain.

But in seconds, I, Felicia Ricci, was in Elphaba's shoes—a living metaphor. I wiggled my toes, carving out my own little space in this legacy of greatness.

"How do they feel?" Amanda asked.

"They feel perfect," I said.

❖   ❖   ❖

I was on a street corner in Manhattan's Battery Park, having walked there from midtown with my best friend Becky. We'd been eating frozen yogurt and distracting each other with scrupulous analysis of the latest celebrity gossip, as was our custom.

There, the phone rang—at precisely 4:55 p.m.—at which point my stomach broke its record for most number of back flips in one 24-hour period.

"Hello?"

"Well, you just fell into a *bowl of jam*," Ann snarled.

"Excuse me?"

Curse you, Annglish!

Pause.

"You got the job, Missy!"

Bingo.

At which point I screamed and leapt into a dance break that was part Running Man, part air guitar. Luckily, New York pedestrians were used to this sort of thing; I think some even tossed over a few nickels.

Still dancing, I put Ann on speaker, and for once, her braying voice was downright mellifluous, layering onto my imaginary dance beat like jelly on musical toast.

Somehow it had happened.

I was going to be in *Wicked*.

And it was time to move to San Francisco.

Later that night I sat cross-legged on the floor of my apartment, having spent the last few hours calling every person who'd ever met me, at whom I shrieked and screamed, sometimes explaining what had happened. Sometimes not.

The gist: *Wicked* had offered me a production contract to perform in the ensemble and understudy the role of Elphaba in their San Francisco company. This company, as well as other national tours in the states and international sit-downs, were satellites of *Wicked*'s Broadway production—so each was produced by the same producers, overseen by the same creative team, and therefore shared the same production values and creative imagining as Broadway.

The icing on my *Wicked* cake? As soon as I signed my contract, I would have the right to join the actors' union, Actor's Equity

Association, making me eligible to attend members-only auditions and later receive health insurance. To signify this, I'd get my very own membership card, a badge to remind me I'd accomplished a once-distant goal.

The sugar flowers on my cake icing? Getting *Wicked* meant no more dreaded day-jobbing.

Hallulejah!

While I'd been chasing the actor dream, I'd been supporting myself marketing medical software, a random job I'd found on Craigslist that taught me the true meaning of suffering. The company was led by a kooky husband and wife team who bickered about power adapters, web browsers, and other mysterious technological things almost every day. They secretly ran their business from a retirement community, using the residential apartment for office space. As such, most mornings when I took the elevator up to the eleventh floor I ran into some poor, incapacitated elder person who was either mumbling about the meaninglessness of life or staring blankly. Which really helped set the appropriate tone for the workday.

But more on that later.

Goodbye, software—hello, Wicked!

I stretched my arms to the ceiling and let out a luxurious, self-congratulatory sigh, recapping the day in my mind.

Of all the phone conversations, my favorite was with my Grandma Yola, a firecracker of an octogenarian who'd seen me in nearly every show I'd ever done, including my very first onstage turn as Young Laurie in *Oklahoma!*, when I danced the famous dream ballet—which, in our version, involved a lot of yawning, both from the actors and the audience. Citing generational bragging rights, Yola promised to call everyone in her phone book to tell them my *Wicked* news, and insist they each do the same, and so on and so forth, into a phone tree of infinity.

"I'm your grandmother. I'm allowed to brag!"

(She said that to me at least once every time I spoke to her.)

Second-favorite call was to gladiator boyfriend Marshall, who stole away to his stairwell at work and whispered that I was the single greatest woman he'd ever known. I told him the same, replacing woman with Gentle Rambo. Moments later he had to get back to work, so we tabled the rest of our conversation. We'd be seeing each other that night to talk—and to figure out what the heck we were going to do, now that I was leaving New York.

Honorable mention went to my mom and dad, mostly because I disproved their theory once and for all that I should go to medical school and be a surgeon. ("You can still sing as a hobby, to your patients, even," my dad would say, which is problematic on many levels, including that a surgeon's patients are unconscious.) But that day they were thrilled—two physicians who could now live vicariously through their artsy-fartsy daughter.

I looked around. The room was quiet. Was there anyone else to call? I heard the faucet drip.

And then, out of nowhere, it happened. The first lightning clap of dread.

Holy crap, what is happening to my life?

I wasn't sure what had sparked it. If I just breathed, I could keep it together.

No, you will not keep it together!

It's a bad sign when I argue with myself in the second person via interior monologue, so I sprinted to my iPod dock and switched on my favorite Early Nineties Mix. This, I knew, would transport me to more carefree, less fashionable times.

You have to move across the country for who knows how long!

So what! Everybody says it'll be like *Full House* twenty-four hours a day.

What's going to happen to you and Marshall?

I cranked the music louder to drown out my thoughts, but did so at the most inconvenient of moments, just as Alanis

Morrisette wailed about rain on my wedding day, which was tragic for obvious reasons, but also for the fact that she was incorrectly illustrating the concept of irony.

It had happened. I'd flipped my excitement coin and it had landed face down. I knew it was only a matter of time before Self-Doubt declared civil war on my Confidence.

Troops mobilized.

They never should have hired you.

I heard the first crack of musket-fire.

You may have been able to fake it at the audition, but you won't be able to fake it onstage.

Cannons raged.

Face it, Felicia: You won't be able to do this.

What, is that a stealth bomber? Are things about to get nuclear?

Incoming!

You. Are. Going. To. FAAAAAAAAAAAIL!

Confidence Soldiers, retreat! Retreeeeeeat!

I collapsed onto my bed and hugged my pillow. The battle was over, but the war would rage on. If I let Self-Doubt win in the end, I'd end up wrecked and ashamed.

And what was I going to do about Marshall?

Several days ago, I'd wandered into my bathroom in the early morning hours to find a miniature yellow envelope wedged at the bottom corner of my medicine cabinet. Inside was a note that said:

I'm falling in love with you. –Marshall

Breathless, I considered the outcomes. Would he earn his own bust, immortalizing our eternal failure? Or would he reveal himself to be the mythical One—that final, missing piece in my Museum Collection?

I was in way over my head.

5. GOODBYE, KANSAS

Email from stage manager David to Felicia.

Hi, Felicia,

Great to talk with you today! A script and score are on the way. Let me know if you want to see the Broadway show (just yourself) and I will check with the Broadway Company Manager.

Cheers, David

Facebook Message from cast member Annie to Felicia.

Hey Felicia! Hear you will be joining us in San Fran! Very exciting. Looking forward to meeting you! if you have any questions don't hesitate. Happy new year and WELCOME!!

Best, Annie

Email from co-company manager Michael to Felicia.

Hi Felicia,

It was nice speaking to you today.

We have a few hotel options if you want to stay in one for a week or so while you look at apartments.

Most of the company have used Craigslist to find their housing out here. We have a few realtors who have helped with corporate housing. Let me know if you want me to put you in touch with them.

Again, Welcome to the Wonderful World of Wicked,
Michael

Facebook Message from theater friend Sam to Felicia.

hey I was in a gift ship today and saw a little wicked witch figurine and was going to get it for you, but then I realized it was going to be expensive to ship it and it was kinda shitty anyway and I just didn't really feel like spending that much and I'd rather get myself some candy.

Love, Sam

It was my last night in New York City. I was commemorating the occasion by eating pizza on the floor, in that way you see people do in movies. Marshall had joined me so we'd ordered a large pie with extra toppings. Apparently, opting for the most possible calories is a good thing when you are trying to double in mass, a favorite practice of men with Adonis-type constitutions. (If you're this Adonis's girlfriend, you run the risk of doing the same.)

(At least my costume fitting was out of the way.)

Marshall had brought with him duct tape, Sharpies, plastic bags, and brute strength for lifting and hauling. We'd been closing up shop all night, pausing at 2 a.m. for a pizza break, reclining on the floor, enjoying our paper-plated Last Supper, until it had somehow become 5 a.m. It felt like the final hours of a sleepover, before the sun started to rise and you heard car doors closing as your parents came to pick you up.

"Looks like we're almost done with everything," said Marshall, folding the empty pizza box in half and stuffing it into a loose black trash bag.

"Way to go," I said, going in for the high five. This I immediately regretted, feeling the lasting sting of his enormous hand on my palm. I often joked with him that he was like the teenage Hercules in the Disney animated movie. Cute and unassuming, he didn't know his own strength, and so brought disaster with him wherever he went—toppling buildings, felling trees. Breaking hearts?

"You have some seasoning or something in the corner of your mouth," he said as he reached toward me with his massive thumb, trying to flick away the tiny morsel, which for him was like threading a needle with a braid of rope.

"There is not a single moment when food is not somewhere on my face," I said.

"Well, I think it's cute," Marshall said, stretching out onto the floor.

Everything about the evening so far had felt heavy and light. Heavy with the finality of change, light with the flutters of anticipation.

I thought back to the past weeks, when the pieces of my new, surreal life had started to come together. I had watched the Broadway production of *Wicked* from the sound booth and also gone in for something called a "wig fitting," during which my head was swathed in cling wrap while a man drew lines and circles on it, like a head topographer. I'd also gotten a Facebook message from a cast member named Annie, an email from Michael, the co-company manager, and David, the stage manager, who sent me the *Wicked* script and score in the mail. One day later I tied up loose ends at my (now former) software job, and one day after that I shipped a giant box of stuff to the Orpheum Theater, *Wicked*'s San Francisco home, full of clothes, books, mementos, and anything else I could fit.

Today it was final goodbyes—to my friends, my brother who lived in Brooklyn, and the rest of my family in Rhode Island. We'd phone-chatted earlier for one last check-in.

"Be careful, Fel," said my dad.

"Take your vitamins!" said my mom.

The only one left was Marshall.

We'd crammed months of dating into three weeks, spending New Year's Eve together in Philadelphia, where we forged new make-out-in-public territory and shared the first midnight kiss I'd ever had with someone who wasn't definitely or probably gay. Afterward we'd stayed a few extra days to visit his family, where we cooked wild duck, watched home videos, and shoveled snow.

I'm falling in love with you. –Marshall

Finding his yellow note that one morning had been a knee-weakening surprise. Although technically I'd brought up the L-word a few days before that—entirely by accident, when we were browsing Borders and sportscaster-commentating on random book titles. Later I noted to Marshall how bookstores were perfect locations for dates, since you could first make fun of everything, then "accidentally" wander into the Kama Sutra section.

"It's a perfect place," I said, "to go with the one you love."

At which point I gasped, then ran away, far into the CD section, where I pretended to be deeply interested in the music of Andrea Bocelli. Since then, the L-word had been hanging in the air—a fat, naked cherub of a word, taunting me with its prickly arrows and pudgy ankles.

Then, a week or two later, I found the note.

In time, there was no denying it: we'd fallen in love, like stupid little idiots.

Because now I had to go.

Stupid!

As I collected the rest of my life into a medium-sized suitcase, I realized I had no idea when I'd be back. Like Elphaba imagining her future in "The Wizard and I," mine too felt "unlimited," in a mysterious, unpredictable way. I felt myself heading toward an impossible challenge, unsure of how (or if) I'd do it, or for how long, or what it would end up feeling like. And soon, everything

I'd known—friends, family, New York, Marshall—would become a shrinking reflection in my rearview mirror.

Goodbye, Kansas.

Marshall and I took a cab to JFK airport. We split a muffin in the food court.

"So. This is it," said Marshall.

"Do you want to just crawl into my carry-on?" I said.

"I do want to do that."

"I think you should do it."

"Okay, I will."

"I mean, aside from the million-dollar plane fares, long distance won't be so bad, right?"

"No, it won't," Marshall said, I think intending to smile. Instead he looked like a caged puppy.

"Actually, I think it might suck," I said.

"Yeah, maybe you are right."

"But we'll find a way," I said, sitting up. "As Jeff Goldblum says in *Jurassic Park*, 'life finds a way.'"

"I love that part. I also love when he bangs the table and yells about selling plastic lunchboxes."

"Oh, you mean this part?"

I reenacted the scene, banging the table in the food court.

"Yes! I love it!"

"The fact that we both love *Jurassic Park* is just one of the reasons why this is going to work out," I said.

"And *The Dark Knight*," added Marshall.

Before long, I was winding through the security line, with no Marshall in my carry-on. Instead, he stood off to the side, keeping watch until I passed the metal detector. Before I turned to go, I looked back and saw him, opening the envelope I'd given him moments before.

Last night I'd written a note of my own. *Bye*, it said. *I'll miss you. You'd better write.* That sort of thing.

And, of course,

I love you, too.

He looked up and beamed, then started waving. I waved back, eyeing his silhouette even as I turned the corner.

6. I AM OZ, THE GREAT AND TERRIBLE

January 11, 2010. Felicia's Blog.

Here I go, writing my first blog post in the thick of the action, aboard Virgin Flight 23, JFK--> SFO. I first want to say that Virgin is tricked out in the style of a very exclusive, very mobile, night club. There is neon purple lighting and the bathrooms play smooth jazz. Although I am not live-blogging right now, the airplane happens to be equipped with free WiFi (no charge for internet but must pay $8 for hummus and carrots). All going well here at 30,000 feet. See you on the ground...

When you wake up in a foreign place, it usually takes a few moments to reacquaint yourself with the facts of your life.

One fact, I soon remembered, was this:

I am going to be in Wicked.

My face curled into a tired smile, at which point I smacked my lips together through morning breath so strong I could smell it on myself.

The next fact?

Marshall wasn't there.

I miss him.

I sighed, then thought that, in a way, it was good he couldn't catch me in this jet-lagged, morning-breath-ridden stupor.

I flopped over on my side, feeling my head pulsing.

Ugh. I hadn't slept well.

Third fact?

My new home was a 10' x 15' room at the Hotel Whitcomb, a medium-rise building across the street from *Wicked*'s theater. I'd booked the hotel for the next two weeks, securing a special company discount. Back in New York, when I'd imagined my future stay here, "hotel" had meant jumping on the bed, ordering room service, and swimming in shallow, reflective pools. But my imagination had gotten a little ahead of itself.

The Whitcomb brooded with a heavy and somber gravitas, like an old-fashioned prison, or any location shot from *The Shining*. Apparently the building had some kind of historical significance I can't really remember. There was something about this on a plaque near its revolving doors, right next to another plaque warning pregnant women that the building could give them cancer.

My room was at the end of the hallway near the elevators, directly next to the ice machine. Being there at first seemed like it would provide a pleasant sense of community, what with people's constant coming and going. But I took it all back last night, as I tossed and turned to the sounds of ice clattering into trays and elevator doors opening and closing every few minutes, accented by the shrill *ding* of the arrival bell.

Still, I knew it was temporary. And at least, come tomorrow, I'd have more important things to worry about than whether I'd run into Jack Nicholson's creepy finger-talking son on his tricycle.

Like being in *Wicked*, for instance.

I was due at work at 1:00 p.m. tomorrow. Today, I had the day to myself.

What to do?

On the airplane ride over, I'd started blogging about my *Wicked* adventures, as a kind of public diary—mostly to get me to sit down and keep track of the experience, and to ensure that Marshall would read it and pine for me from afar. That morning I drafted a quick follow-up post from my hotel room, then decided to head out and explore the city.

Because I have an abysmal sense of direction, closely akin to a baby's, I thought it wise to allot most of the day to getting a handle on my surroundings. Even though *Wicked*'s theater was across the street, it would not be unheard of for me to get lost the next day on the way there, wandering into, say, the state of Washington.

I trotted out of the lobby onto Market Street, a well-known landmark whose name, to me, evoked commerce, industry, and progress. I'd been to San Francisco twice before (when I was peddling medical software, actually, for the dreaded day job), so I knew all about how this central thoroughfare cut through the entire city, from South West to North East.

How brilliant that Wicked's *theater sits on this illustrious street,* I thought to myself, in a strangely formal interior voice.

Stalling on the red brick sidewalk, my first instinct was to turn left—so I turned right, since when it comes to directions my first instinct is usually the opposite of how one should proceed. After a few strides I felt the wind whip across my neck, and so zipped up my coat and burrowed my face in my scarf. As I would soon discover, San Francisco's weather had a daily identity crisis, unable to commit to hot or cold. Its air was dry, fleeting, impossible to hold onto, two-faced in the shadow and the light. That afternoon it was cloudy with patches of sun and gusts of frigid wind—an upgrade from New York winter, but certainly not what I'd pictured as sunny California.

I crossed the first intersection next to the hotel as the *Wicked* marquee glided past me on my left, a road sign beckoning me to veer off and approach. But I pressed on, maybe because I was intimidated, maybe because I knew that the theater and I would become acquainted soon enough. I eyed it as I zipped by, making note of its location, then soldiering on—a latter-day Magellan on a mission of discovery.

But I am a terrible explorer. A few feet more and I felt the first pang of hunger, soon realizing that every pioneer needs food in her stomach and a manicure on her fingernails. Although not necessarily both at the same time.

While I rarely get my nails done under normal circumstances, in times of upheaval nothing melts my cares away like money and time-wasting luxuries. While going through one of my breakups with Matt 3.0, I dropped more cash on gossip magazines than groceries, and bought at least six different kinds of sunhats, even though it was winter.

Mani-pedis reminded me of best friend Becky, so I decided to give her a quick call.

"Becks?"

"Son!"

"Hey, son!"

"Son, are you gone?"

"Yeah, son, I'm in San Fran! Can you even believe it?"

(We call each other "son." I do not know why.)

As we chatted, I scanned the nearby blocks, spotting only a Burger King and a fast food place called "Carl's Jr." where there was a picture of a hamburger and a star with a smiley face. I continued past a big plaza that stretched from *Wicked*'s theater all the way to the end of the block. On it was a raised patch of grass, enclosed in a low, single-chain suggestion of a fence. On the far end, opposite the grass, was a homely fountain, constructed from blocks of concrete and other right-angled shapes. I crossed the street to this large lot, eager to find somewhere to eat and/or get my nails painted jungle red.

"So, let's talk outfits," said Becky.

Becky had a Masters in journalism, and was a pro at extracting a ton of information from me in a short amount of time. Only a couple of minutes in and already we were bouncing around ideas for what I should wear the next day, to dazzle everyone with my (feigned) sense of fashion.

"Actually, I looked in my suitcase," I said, "and I'm worried I shipped all my good clothes separately, with UPS. All I really have is my travel dress."

My travel dress was a black muu-muu that swung loosely from my shoulders, perfect for hiding things beneath it, like small children, or a bad body image.

"Okay, but make sure you belt it."

Becky was right; I looked less like an old lady in a housedress when I belted it.

By this point I was standing right next to the fountain, getting sprayed with misty city water. On this side of the street, everything seemed darker, dingier, in need of a good scrubbing. A guitar started playing somewhere. I turned toward the sound and noticed a cluster of people singing and swaying behind the patch of grass, swigging from a bottle and sticking out their tongues. One of them, a man, had a metal sword and was sparring with an invisible opponent.

"What's wrong?" said Becky. "You got quiet."

"Nothing," I said, "except I just spotted a man sword fighting with the air."

"Oh, I should have assumed."

As I hustled down the block, Becky asked me whether or not I was nervous about starting *Wicked*.

"Obviously, I am nervous," I said. "I mean I have no idea what I'm doing."

"Please, that is so not true," said Becky, launching into her patented, two-minutes-or-less best friend pep talk.

As Becky reminded me of my "baller G-dom," I kept scanning my surroundings, looking for somewhere, anywhere to duck inside. But there were only pawn, sex, and discount shops, like the cheap squares on some depressing, adult-themed Monopoly board. In the next ten minutes, I dodged five different piles of poo, the advances of an old woman wearing one shoe and carrying the other, and a Raggedy Andy-haired man who tipped over every trash can on the sidewalk, singing "London Bridge Is Falling Down."

In that same short amount of time, Becky had gotten me to confess my deepest insecurities—most notably my belief that, in being cast in *Wicked*, I'd been set up to fail. It was only a matter of time, I thought, before everybody found out the truth—maybe as soon as tomorrow.

"You are insane," said Becky.

"Like, I took the job, so I agreed I could play Elphaba. But, honestly? I'm pretty sure I did a bad thing."

"That is just the Catholic guilt talking. What's wrong?"

"What?"

"You just gasped."

"Oh, yeah, a lady grabbed my arm and told me to give her my coffee, even though I am carrying no coffee."

"What the hell is going on over there?"

"Honestly, Becks, I don't know."

What *was* this Godforsaken place? This was not the San Francisco I knew from *Full House*. I ducked my head down and started power walking like a high-strung soccer mom.

"I'd better go," I said. "I may need both hands to defend myself."

"Yeah, I gotta go, too. I'm meeting Millhouse for a drink in Harlem."

Becky called her boyfriend Millhouse because he looked like that character from *The Simpsons*.

"Have fun."

"You too! Be safe. And good luck!"

As I hung up the phone, I saw it—like a mirage emerging from the wasteland. On the horizon were tall spires with flags stretching into the sky, announcing the presence of a giant shopping mall. Inside its fortress of window shops were an expansive food court and—glory be!—a beauty salon. Not to mention loads of kiosks with ghetto bling and wide-rim hats. Maybe a diamond grill to go with my red nails and muu-muu?

After sprinting inside, I felt the cool rush of air conditioning on my already freezing body. In the Food Court I loaded up on smoothies and General Tso's kitchen, before enjoying a full-bellied manicure while reading *Us Weekly* magazine.

I think that's enough exploring for one day, I thought to myself.

On my way back, I took a cab.

7. FIRST DAY OF SCHOOL

From the street, *Wicked*'s stage door looked like any other door, except for the fact that it was the width of a car and had STAGE DOOR written on it—so actually it was not at all like other doors. It sat squarely at the long edge of the theater, next to a painted mural of *Wicked*'s logo, the iconic image of a blithe and blonde Glinda whispering something to Elphaba, whose eyes were obscured, her mouth curling into a smirk.

Weary from yesterday's sidewalk safari, at 12:54 p.m. I made a beeline for the theater, keeping my eye on the mural, hoping to outrun the drunken, shoeless, sword-wielding street folk. Dressed in a belted muu-muu, I arrived at the pair of utility doors, my cotton tote in one hand, my crumpled rehearsal schedule in the other, feeling like an overgrown kindergartener on her first day of school. There was no one waiting outside, so I reached for the handle, pulled, and walked in. Easy enough.

Kindergarten shouldn't be too bad!

I stepped into a small and deserted vestibule that felt kind of like an entryway to a warehouse, with crates to my right and miscellaneous boxes stacked below a bulletin board. Gazing further I saw black draped fabric, and another doorway ahead. I started toward the bulletin board, then heard a voice,

"Can I help you?"

I turned. The voice had come from a large man sitting and watching television in what looked like a closet, directly to the left of the doors.

"Hi!" I said.

"Can I help you?"

"Uh, I'm here for *Wicked*."

"Name."

"Felicia Ricci?"

He glanced down at his folding table.

"Let me call David."

In the silence I turned back to the bulletin board, where I spotted a digital clock, ticking down the seconds, and many handouts: company news, a backstage guest policy, a sign about something called the "Birthday Club," a notice about health and hand washing. There was also what appeared to be a sign-in sheet, with a hanging pencil on a string. On this sheet were thirty-odd names, those of *Wicked*'s cast members—my soon-to-be coworkers. Next to it, pinned in the center, was the same weekly schedule I was clutching in my fist, which David, the stage manager, had forwarded to me in an email. I'd read it over so many times, I nearly had it memorized.

WICKED SAN FRANCISCO
Rehearsal/Performance Schedule | January 11-17, 2010
First Rehearsal: Felicia Ricci

Below the heading were rehearsal dockets for each day, Tuesday through Sunday, with a performance count for that day.

TUES 1/12
Performance #1204

And in the rehearsal column:

Stage Manager's Office
1:00p-1:30p Orientation w/ David: Felicia Ricci

Wardrobe
1:30p-2:30p Wardrobe Fitting: Felicia Ricci

Vocal Rehearsal Room
2:30p-4:30p Vocals w/ Steve: Felicia Ricci

Hair Room
6:00p-7:00p Fitting: Felicia Ricci

According to the digital clock, I had fifteen seconds until orientation began.

"Felicia," I heard somebody say. I spun around to see a man of medium build with short, dark hair approaching with his hand extended.

"David Lober, production stage manager."

I looked at the digital clock. He was almost exactly on time, with four seconds to spare.

"David! Nice to meet you."

"I see you've found our callboard and call sheet."

I nodded. "I love this illustrated handout about health and hand washing."

"The call sheet is where you'll sign in every day. Follow me."

As I followed David several yards inside and down one flight of stairs, I admired his take on the patterned button-down, tucked conscientiously into his day jeans, which sported a neutral belt.

He wore a thin shell necklace, which, from the front, peeked out from his open collar, glistening as it caught the light. It was an outfit for the weekday that hadn't forgotten the weekend.

When we reached the basement there was a table with a microwave; many disposable utensils, cups, and bowls; hanging papers; and announcement sheets taped to the wall.

"Is the rest of the cast around?" I asked as we turned the corner and headed through the first doorway, to what looked like David's office.

"Not today. Since Monday is our day off, Tuesday is still kind of like our 'weekend.' We don't usually schedule anything before 7:30 p.m. But for you, we make the exception."

I laughed like a hyena.

"Lucky me!"

David was already seated at his desk, so instead of doing that thing where you punch someone's arm, I slapped my own knee, like a banjo player counting off the first bars of her song.

"All right, so here is your folder of materials."

He handed me a green pocket folder, the exact kind I used to use for homework assignments.

Kindergarten is the best!

"This should give you a pretty good overview of how things are done."

Each handout boasted *Wicked*'s logo at the top, while some said SAN FRANCISCO in huge letters down the side. One listed our performance schedule (one show every night at 8 p.m., matinees on Wednesday and Sunday at 2 p.m.), while another enumerated nearby pharmacies, public transportation, and suggested "points of interest," including an Asian Art Museum and something called the Exploratorium.

Next there was a sheet that said, *Individual Track: Felicia Ricci (3F)*.

"Here you'll see a breakdown of your ensemble track, or part," David said. "It lists your scenes, the location you enter from, the solo lines you're responsible for, where you exit, and any notes to take into consideration. Of course, you'll learn this in the weeks to come, from Kirsten and Allison, our dance captain and her assistant."

My eyes darted across the page, whose code was indecipherable: horizontal lines of text along a matrix of numbers and shorthand phrases. It read like modern poetry, and/or a transcript of two people playing Battleship:

Thank Goodness, R1 (Prosc. Stairs), "I hear that she can shed her skin as easily as a snake!" *L2, to Ballroom, L3, book (give to Selma), L3, to Party QC – gondola...*

I decided I needed to back things up, and so asked eloquently,

"So, I'll be, like, rehearsing with just two people—like, on my own?"

"Right. Our dance captains will teach you your material individually. You'll have a few chances to rehearse with some other cast members, but that comes later. Then it'll be time for your put-in."

He explained how a put-in was basically a one-person dress rehearsal—the final step before joining the cast.

"And what about the Elphaba stuff?" I asked.

"Oh, we won't be getting into Elphaba until after you've been put into the ensemble, which will be on..." his voice trailed as he glanced down, "February 5th. Then we'll rehearse you during the day while you perform at night."

I shuffled back a few more sheets, to one with thirty little photos, labeled with each cast member's name and his or her role in the company. As I skimmed, I saw one labeled *Teal Wicks – Elphaba,* then two rows up, *Vicki Noon – Standby for Elphaba.*

"I have one other question," I said. "And I don't mean to jump the gun here—but what's a standby? I see here it says 'Standby for Elphaba.' Is that like an understudy? Are there two Elphaba understudies?"

"Right. Vicki is our standby, so she is basically our first understudy to Elphaba, taking over for Teal whenever she's out. When Vicki is not on as Elphaba, she doesn't perform in the show, in any ensemble track. She 'stands by.' You, on the other hand, are our Elphaba *understudy*, which means you're in the ensemble, and you'll go on for Elphaba when both Teal and Vicki are out."

"Ah, I see. Cool."

My throat caught. I wasn't sure why. This was good news, right? With two people covering the role, being understudy meant much less pressure—because I might not ever have to play Elphaba. I mean, what were the odds? Plus, I'd get to be in the ensemble each night, as part of the company.

David rose to lead me on my first backstage tour. Outside his office we veered to the right, past the folding tables with their Styrofoam and plastic artifacts, then rounded the bend to a long hallway, where there was a wall of peoples' faces. Each photo had been mounted inside clipart frames that read,

I left my heart (and brains and courage) in San Francisco

"These are cast members who have left the company since it opened over two years ago," David said.

I spotted a photo of Eden Espinosa in the center, a legendary former Elphaba. She was making a cartoony "frowny" face and waving at the camera.

"Eden Espinosa performed here in San Francisco?" I asked.

"She was our Elphaba in the Los Angeles company, which is technically the same company you're now a part of."

"Right. Forgot about that."

"From Los Angeles to San Francisco. Quite a group."

I looked at David and smiled, noting his glimmer of sentimentality, no matter how understated.

We continued down the hallway, wandering past a series of dressing room doors, on which there were laminated signs with actor and character names that I recognized from the bios and headshots I'd seen on *Wicked*'s website. In passing, these signs began to spell out *Wicked*'s story—*Madame Morrible* and *Nessarose* in the first hallway, an alcove for *Boq*, *The Wizard*, *Fiyero* and *Doctor Dillamond*. They were names I had once known as an audience member, then later as an actor studying her script, and which I'd soon know in the flesh—as a *peer*.

At the end of the hallway were the ensemble dressing rooms. We peeked into the girls'. It was modestly sized and carpeted, with a center partition dividing the room into three sections. Exposed pipe peeked from the office tile ceiling, and wrapping around the border of the room were mirrors and vanity light bulbs on a dimmer, with one long, built-in table stretching along the wall. This table was subdivided into stations, with a chair placed every few feet. Above the mirror were names of the cast members who had claimed that slice of real estate.

Littering the stations were trinkets and accessories, windows into each girl's personality. At one, a mini bonsai fountain, at another, a makeup trunk so large it looked like luggage. Photos, postcards, and post-its were stuck here and there—evidence of life, paused for now—restarting in a moment's time. A city, deserted.

I knew it was only a matter of time before I'd know what all of it meant, how it all worked—when staring at this room would feel less like piecing together some Indiana Jones-type mystery, and more like the simple, mundane routine of going to work.

When I'd feel like one of *them*.

A part of *Wicked*.

❖   ❖   ❖

"Next, we went upstairs, to check out the wings."

It was my dinner break, and I'd called my mom to debrief her on the events of the day so far. I was sitting in the bathtub, the only place in my hotel room that got cell service, where I'd fashioned a back cushion from a rolled-up sweatshirt.

"What are 'the wings?'"

I explained to my mom how the "wings" immediately surrounded the stage. It was where actors hung out right before they walked on, stagehands rearranged the set, and dressers did quick changes.

"Did you get to go onstage?" asked my mother.

"Yep! I walked all the way across."

I told my mom how the stage was not black like you might imagine, but the color of wood, and riddled with metal tracks for set pieces, little speaker monitors that play the orchestra audio for the actors, and panels that sprayed special effect smoke, fog, and wind.

"That's amazing," said my mother.

By her coaxing, soon I had launched into a Backstage Tour "Greatest Hits," if you will, which I shall obviously transcribe here for your reading pleasure.

Presenting,

Backstage Tour Greatest Hits!
Brought to you by Felicia's Interior Monologue

1) *It takes a lot of crap to put on a show.*

The vast array of objects I came across on my tour felt like clues which, when assembled, told their own version of *Wicked*—that of its other life, unseen. Part wonderland, part Home Depot, part teacher lounge, the environment was impossible to categorize.

As David led me around, I realized that the theater was organized into two main levels. The props, set pieces, big production element-type stuff, and the stage itself were on the top level, with mostly everything else in the basement (dressing rooms, storage space, costume rooms, and wig rooms). Stage left and right in the wings held shelving units for the show's props—Glinda's crystal staff, schoolbooks for the Ozian students, tickets to the Emerald City's "Wizomania" show, a disconcertingly lifelike green baby—each of which had its own meticulously chosen space, where it resided at all times except when needed onstage.

Lining the basement and dotting parts of the upstairs wings were garment racks holding dozens upon dozens of costumes—almost as if the New York costume shop had been broken into pieces and reshuffled into the theater. Wherever there was space, there was a garment rack—outside the bathroom, near the stage management office, at the foot of the stage right stairwell. It seemed it was the only way to accommodate a costume-heavy show into a fairly confined space.

In the remaining nooks and crannies were hints of humanity: lunch containers, facedown paperback books, water bottles, First Aid kits, lip balm—tools used by the villagers who inhabited this unpredictable landscape.

2) Whoa... technical stuff!

Singers warmed up their voices, dancers stretched their limbs, *Wicked's* stage crew prepared and maintained. Every once in a while during the tour a burly man in a black shirt would appear, attaching doo-dads to thing-a-ma-hoosits, placing fabric sheets over rolling doo-hickeys. Theater tech was one aspect of student and amateur theater that I never fully, or even partially, understood—so when it came to the big leagues, seeing *Wicked*'s technical inner workings felt like I was bearing witness to miracles. Each time a black-shirted burly man walked by, he did his thing with such a sense of purpose and quick skill that I almost wanted to kneel out of respect.

3) *Lots of giant heavy things are hanging over my head.*

As I was admiring the confounding rope-pully mechanisms in the wings, I soon realized that there were many giant things hanging directly over my head, almost fifty feet in the air.

("What!" said my mother.

I could practically hear her hyperventilating over the phone.

"Mom, don't worry," I said.

"I *will* worry," she said.)

During the tour, David had taken a moment to explain how *Wicked*'s scenic design worked. Most of the medium-to-large set pieces—from the somewhat-manageable to the downright unwieldy (giant staircases, flaming pillars of fire)—were strung up on wires, hooks, and pulleys, and hoisted high into the air by the stage crew. Before, during, and after the show, the crew had to perform an elaborate set-change dance—their takedown or hoist-up sequence choreographed alongside the cast's traffic patterns, perfectly timed to accommodate the show's scenery needs.

It was pretty amazing. But, as an unfortunate consequence, a giant set piece would be hanging over my (and everybody's) head—more or less at all times.

4) *The wig room is creepy.*

After leaving the stage and crossing downstairs, David and I peeked inside something called the wig room, where I saw a bunch of blank, disembodied heads. On those heads were wigs in the most ridiculous styles I'd ever seen: wavy mullets and curly updos, many of which were woven around wiring that looked like painful orthodontic headgear. There were curlers, hairnets, and bottles of gel and hairspray, all of which were used to sculpt and set the wigs in between shows.

The heads were faceless but I could imagine their rolling eyes, their *tssk*ing mouths. It was not so much that I found the heads unnerving as I found their wigs to be scarily realistic, giving each of them a distinctive personality—and, in turn, a story.

What had that curly red one witnessed? Had the traffic cone updo been in the original Broadway cast? Did Sideburn Braids gossip with Pink Beret?

Backstage at a show is a dangerous place for a girl with a wild imagination. As I was surrounded by such intricate craftsmanship, the magical world of *Wicked* almost subsumed the real world, blending fantasy and reality.

5) *Is that room a closet?*

I'm not sure how things are backstage in theaters the world over, but at the Orpheum many spaces that might conventionally warrant four walls, a ceiling, and a door, had (for whatever reason) been placed in closets. Room taxonomy isn't always clear, so it was hard to tell, but I was pretty sure that many "rooms" were, indeed, straight-up broom-holdin', shoe-rackin' closets.

Rooms up for debate:

A. The security guard's little man cave directly inside the stage door, which was too small to fit anything but a human and his TV tray.

B. The vocal rehearsal room, which stood adjacent to the stage right stairs. This "room" was a small, Harry Potter-esque hideaway that doubled as an office space for Bryan, the conductor and music director. Along with its upright piano, couch, hanging Japanese lantern, and poster of a shirtless man, there were granola bars and other provisions piled in the corner. If not a closet, it could have also been a hideaway for fugitives or changelings, if they were musically inclined and into shirtless dudes.

C. Lastly, there was the physical therapy room, big enough only for a stretch table and a chair. I think the only space from my past that rivaled the physical therapy room in preposterous smallness was my freshman year dorm room, which I shared with a laundry-flinging yell-talker named Erin. There were other similarities, too. Both closet-rooms had terrible wall art (dorm— bookstore-bought French print; therapy—*Mama Mia!* poster) and were places where people suffered in silence.

6) *To be a male cast member, you must be confident.*

While everyone in the ensemble was assigned a communal dressing room like the one I'd visited earlier, there were extra dressing areas throughout the basement and upper level for more rapid, mid-show costume changes. The women's areas were called *gondolas* and were encased in black hanging fabric. The men's weren't called anything, and stood shamelessly out in the open. Which is to say: the men changed in front of everybody. Like tribesmen splaying their goods in the underbrush.

You've got to admire that kind of confidence.

("Are you being serious?" asked my mother.

"I *am* being serious," I said.)

Luckily (or unluckily, depending on your perspective) nobody was ever required to strip down to less than a t-shirt and underwear.

("Well, thank goodness for *that*," she said.)

Amidst my mother's expressions of incredulity, pleasure, and concern, I rounded out my Greatest Hits with a list of miscellaneous actor perks, with special mention of the bins of free cough drops scattered about, the water coolers and mini cups on either side of the stage, and the fact that somebody offered discount Pilates classes to cast members on certain afternoons.

"And how did your rehearsal go?" asked my dad, who apparently had been listening on another line (he does that sometimes).

"Oh, hi, Dad," I said. "It went pretty well."

After my backstage tour, I'd had a brief costume fitting—followed by my first ever *Wicked* vocal rehearsal, during which I thankfully didn't implode or start weeping from the stress.

It was led by Steve, assistant music director and associate conductor. In addition to being an awesome pianist, Steve confirmed my suspicions that at some point quirky authority figures decided they should all wear round-framed glasses (a suspicion I first had while under the instruction of Yale professors). Tall and blonde with a *Where's Waldo* gleam in his sometimes-glassy, sometimes-cutting gaze, Steve was a curious blend of laid-back California and old-fashioned curmudgeon. During our rehearsal I first thought I'd charmed him, but later I was nitpicked like a lice-ridden monkey. Chuckling one moment, snapping about the rigors of breathing, consonants, and phrasing the next, Steve was the principal who would stage a school prank with you, then suspend you for it.

I had painstakingly learned all of my ensemble vocals once I'd received my script and score back in New York; I expected *extra* gold stars, since I'd practically memorized everything.

But Steve was unfazed. Noting only,

"Teaching you shouldn't be too bad."

He then proceeded to stop me every five seconds—to discuss diction, vowels, crescendos—the works.

I soon got to know some of the show's more idiosyncratic musical direction. Like every time I sang "witch of the west" Steve said it needed to be "witch-a-the-west," and that "one short day" should actually be "one shore day" when sung in unison. Not only that, but every held note had a precise cutoff that had to be memorized—meaning double memorization duty for every song. I had never before encountered such detailed musical direction.

"You must be smaaaht," said my dad, parodying a Rhode Island accent—a recurring bit of his.

"Well, we'll see. I mean it was only my first day."

"What do you mean, 'we'll see?' You're gorgeous and talented," said my mother, her mother lioness mane bristling. If she ever senses a hint of insecurity, her tactic is to pounce on her children with a flurry of direct, if not irrelevant, compliments.

"I know, Mom, I wasn't putting myself down."

"You could play Elphaba *and* Glinda, you're so talented!"

"Okay, thanks, Mom, but I am not playing Glinda."

"But you could! You could sing it! And you're gorgeous!" my mother yelled.

(It is a characteristic of Riccis to yell as if in argument when we're actually saying mundane or even encouraging things to each other.

Example *(read as shouted)*:

MOM: WASH YOUR HANDS BEFORE COMING INTO THE KITCHEN!

FELICIA: DID YOU GET THE MAIL?

DAD: LOOK AT ALL THOSE CATALOGS!
FELICIA: DON'T THROW AWAY MY MAGAZINES!
DAD: WHY IS THE STOVE ON LOW? BRING THE WATER TO
A BOIL FIRST, THEN TURN IT DOWN!
MOM: YOU LOOK NICE TODAY!
DAD: YOU DO, TOO!
FELICIA: HEY, I GOT AN A ON MY PHYSICS TEST!
MOM AND DAD: YOU'RE A GENIUS!)

"Anyway, I have to go," I said, unrolling my sweatshirt and climbing out of the tub. "Tonight I'm going to meet the cast and watch the show."

I looked in the bathroom mirror at my belted muu-muu, bird's nest hair, and chapped colorless lips.

I hope the other kids like me.

"Well, have fun, sweetie, and call us any time," said my mom, coming down from her compliment frenzy.

I said goodbye to my parents and gathered my things, resisting the urge as I headed out the door to call home once again—to ask one final question.

Will you come drop me off at school, Mommy?

❖   ❖   ❖

In the one-and-a-half minutes it took David to lead me down the hall to the girls' dressing room, the version of me that was cool, collected—*modern marvel able to leap social barriers in a single bound*—still existed. In those moments, I still stood a chance of being totally agreeable, or, if we're aiming high, likeable.

Soon I heard a soft stream of hip-hop music coming from the doorway. I fiddled with my belt, tipped my head back, and put on an expression that oozed warmth and friendliness. One that said,

"Nice to meet you, coworkers!" Yes, my plan was to act like a Disney park employee.

David knocked on the door with his knuckles.

"Ladies? Everybody decent?"

Soon we were standing inside the doorway, amidst the pulsing music—louder now—thumping with my heartbeat, while I stood, grinning so wide it tingled.

"This is Felicia, everybody!"

And there I saw civilization, enlivened, filled with people, coming at me in droves.

"Hey there!" "Hello!" "What's up?" "How's it going?" everybody chorused back. I tried to match voices to faces but could see only twelve or more people-pillars, with eyes, ears, mouths—all the appropriate parts—somehow impossible to differentiate.

It's just nerves.

Finally, I stepped forward, in my dazzling muu-muu, and introduced myself.

"Hi, I'm Felicia," I said, brilliantly.

One by one, with nylon wig caps stretched across their heads, girls began materializing from the crowd.

"I'm Annie," chirped one, her hair looped in curls. Her smile was wide, like a double-decker bus, square and stacked taller than seemed possible.

"Annie, hi! Thanks for the Facebook message!"

"I'm Kristen, nice to meet you."

"Allison, hi."

"I'm Alexa," said another girl with platinum hair and large breasts who sat next to,

"Laura, nice to meet you," another girl with large breasts, who sat next to,

"Fiama! Welcome to the cast," a slightly older woman with large breasts.

Laura, the one in the middle, was the girl I'd be replacing in the ensemble.

"We get to sit next to each other," confirmed blonde Alexa, in a high-pitched voice.

"Penelope!" "Neka!" "Kehau!"

The roll call continued, kind of like that scene from *The Sound of Music* when all the kids marched forward and shouted their names.

A few minutes into the meet and greet, and it was smooth sailing. I struck up a conversation with Fiama about her husband and young son, mostly to divert my roaming eyes, which kept getting drawn down almost magnetically to the enormous breasts that surrounded me. When it would come time for me to sit among this well-endowed middle row, my own chest was going to look like the only two guppies in a sea of marlins, the only two raisins at the grapefruit stand, the only two (you get the idea).

Still, I was filled with hope. At *Wicked* I could write my own story. Now there was Alexa, Fiama, Neka, Penelope—my new maybe-friends, whose names all by coincidence ended in vowels and sounded vaguely royal.

Who would care that growing up I'd never been so great with the "popular crowd?" That I had a tendency to clam up socially, to go at things on my own, to shy away from others? And what did it matter that everybody here was super-cool, successful, and outrageously attractive? That the dressing room could have been a holding cell for the earth's most diverse and exhaustive collection of beautiful specimens? (We're not talking "hot girls" here; we're talking women who cause heads to turn and fashion-challenged individuals to tingle with a conflicting mixture of jealousy and hero-worship. Not that I knew what that was like.)

Whatever the outcome, so far, on my first day, I felt like I'd arrived. All the mystery, the piecing together, the wondering about who to be, had been overwrought.

The words that Julie had spoken during our coaching session floated back to me.

She's brave, and sticks her neck out.

It was true.

And if Elphaba could do it, so could I.

8. THE TIMES THEY ARE A-CHANGIN'

January 13, 2010. Felicia's Blog.

When one is inserted into a pre-existing company, the first few weeks of rehearsal are, in a word, insane. In, like, a good way, but also in a way that makes me want to hide under a rock.

Since I am a replacement cast member, my staging rehearsal has involved the dance captain playing all the other people's roles around me while I try to map out my particular pathways along a grid (there are numbers across the front of the stage to describe stage L versus stage R, and then there are other markings to determine depth of my position).

Without getting into the nitty-gritty, let me just say that today really made me appreciate just how precise and detail-oriented *Wicked* is. There is, of course, room for interpretation -- and, dare I say, acting! -- but everything from a head flick to the angle of one's stance is evaluated for its clarity of expression and cohesiveness with the whole. Musical theater is a veritable playground for those with OCD-like tendencies!

I need to go shower now because, well -- based the grueling nature of the past two days of rehearsal, I'm sure you can extrapolate just how often I've been able to shower.

Cleanly,
Felicia.

I had done it: survived my first two weeks of rehearsal.

The main challenge didn't so much stem from the fact that the days were long (which they were), but that I was learning the entirety of *Wicked* by myself. On a good day, one or two cast members might lend me some of their time, running around, playing a combination of parts, sporadically reciting lines or singing harmonies, while I wandered around in confusion to the damp underscoring of a lone upright piano.

But more often than not, it was just me and the dance captains, Kristen and Allison, who took me under their wings like weary and reluctant governesses in a Victorian novel. As *Wicked* veterans and keepers of its blocking, each had memorized all the "tracks" (or parts) in the show, from the ensemble to the lead characters, teaching incoming cast members their every step, twirl, and gesture, down to the most minute, painstaking detail. Not only that: in addition to teaching, they were incredible performers—subbing in for members of *Wicked*'s ensemble on a near-nightly basis.

Mostly I was obsessed with the fact that you could (in theory) walk up to either of them, shout a moment from *Wicked*, and they could perform it for you, as any character, right before your tired, glossy eyes, while you did a slow clap and gave them accuracy scores. (This never actually happened, but sometimes I dreamed of doing it as a party game.)

On the bright side, I was done with my two-week stint of living in the hospitality hell known as the Hotel Whitcomb. Bidding goodbye to the specter of Jack Nicholson, his Big Wheel-riding son, and the flesh-and-blood maids who cleaned my room at 8 a.m. (if and *only if* I put out my *Do Not Disturb* sign), I finally schlepped my suitcase and cardboard box to a modest studio apartment in San Francisco's Mission District, which lay south of *Wicked*'s theater. This, by everyone's account, would be a truly happening neighborhood—providing much-needed relief from the psychological injury incurred by doing hard time on Market Street (campus for the public urinators and coffee-snatchers).

But, alas. My first evening in the Mission I walked by a man playing a broken-stringed guitar and singing about the evils of sodomy. A few blocks later, a woman emerged, completely drenched, holding a mattress and yelling at the top of her lungs. Soon she was coughing and sputtering in my face, and wouldn't stop spitting until I'd ducked around the corner.

"Wait, what?" Marshall said, gasping. I could see his face contorting on my computer screen, next to the time ticker of our Skype chat that read 74 minutes. We'd been doing the long-distance thing, and so had become obsessed with talking via webcam.

"It's all true," I said. "Everyone who has visited San Francisco must be in on some conspiracy; they all say it's amazing, but no matter where I go, something outrageous happens to me."

"Should I be worried, Fel? Are you safe?"

"Sure, I'm safe. I think I just, like, need a car. Or an electric scooter."

"A Segway! You should get one and also wear a giant helmet. For safety."

"I need *some* kind of vehicle to get around. Everybody in the cast who has a car appears to be really happy."

"But isn't there public transportation?" asked Marshall as he sipped from a stout glass of Bourbon. (On Skype date night Marshall went all-out, while I abstained in the service of vocal health, sipping lemon water from a straw.)

I explained to Marshall how in San Francisco "public transportation" was a term used loosely. Everything was so spread out and scattered that after you took a train or bus, you'd end up having to walk really far to your end destination anyway, up and down the steep hills. In the meantime, you'd have no choice but to faceoff with the army of insanity. In short, "public transportation" worked best for people who didn't actually have anywhere to go.

"I could be your car," volunteered Marshall, taking a generous sip of booze and swirling it in his mouth. "I'll carry you."

"Okay, deal. Are you gas or hybrid?"

"Hybrid."

"You run on peanut butter and string cheese."

(These were two of his favorite foods. I know, you don't have to tell me—I'm *so* good at flirting.)

"Anyway," I said, recovering, "I'm really excited for next month."

Marshall and I had been planning his first visit for weeks now. He'd even bought his plane ticket to San Francisco New Year's Eve weekend, when I'd been visiting his family. Orbitz.com had never seemed so romantic.

"I'm excited, too!"

I began listing a bunch of stuff around the city that we had to visit—the Ferry Building, Fisherman's Wharf, the Aquarium—when, suddenly, something possessed me to say,

"Seriously? When you come out and visit, you should just stay."

Marshall snickered, loose from the Bourbon. "I know, I totally should."

"I mean, think about it," I said, indulging in the fantasy, "you could just shack up with me. It would be like summer camp. You don't like your job, so that would be a way out, and you could spend your time here deciding what you really want to do."

The more I thought about it, the more it seemed to make sense. Marshall had been having career doubts since before I'd met him. He'd been working at an e-commerce website that sold men's pants, where he did their customer service and wrote a style blog (on which, incidentally, I'd started commenting as my male alter ego, Phil Yeesh). Life had been plodding along for him, but from what he'd told me, something was missing. Still, he kept his nose to the grindstone.

"That would be so crazy," he said, his eyes lighting up.

Marshall and I loved entertaining what-if scenarios, hypothesizing their outcomes to the fullest extent. In the past, we'd tackled such quandaries as, *What if we lived in a barn that was also a post-apocalyptic bunker?* (Conclusion: It would be awesome.) *What if Marshall were Hugh Jackman for a day?* (Conclusion: It would be awesome.)

"Seriously, Marsh, you should just do it," I said, ever the lemon water-sipping temptress. "You can be my deadbeat boyfriend for a while, find a part-time job, then figure out whatever the next step will be."

"Ha ha. Well, at least I could cook for you! And carry you everywhere."

"Marsh, I am serious," I said, not knowing if I was serious, but worried that I was, and he wasn't.

"Me too," he said.

"Okay, good. We agree."

"It's happening."

"I know it is."

Like all of our other hypotheticals, we concluded that it would be awesome.

But the really funny thing? This one actually came true.

❖   ❖   ❖

Before Marshall arrived, I lived alone in a building called "The Hunky House," a three-story townhouse so-named after its landlord—who was the opposite of hunky but whose last name was Hunkiwiecz (hence, "Hunky").

Four other *Wicked* company members lived there. Tim, a jolly broad-shouldered man with a shaved head, lived upstairs with his Pilates-instructor wife and two extremely Scandinavian-looking children. He was a long-time cast member who played Elphaba's father and, while exceedingly jovial, felt less like a friend than a camp counselor trying to get me excited about arts and crafts. Maybe it was the age gap.

Next there was Tom, our Wizard, a delightful man whom I first knew from his role in the movie *The Birdcage* (which I'd memorized in my youth). He lived downstairs and worked out at the gym down the street.

Directly across the hallway was fellow newbie Etai, who was rehearsing to take over the role of Boq (the small, overlooked munchkin) a week after I would join the cast. With an infectious laugh and brown eyes that curved into half-moon smiles, the boy called Etai BenShlomo—whose name was *not* the punch line to an ethnic joke—was a little ray of aggressive sunshine. He'd been born a full-on Israeli and his mother was a physical therapist, which meant both that he exclaimed things in Hebrew and was always grabbing peoples' shoulders, giving massage tutorials, and explaining the merits of back-cracking. (It is also worth noting that only by coincidence, as opposed to its actor's religious obligation, did the character of Boq's costume include a *yarmulke-esque* skull cap.)

Lastly, there was stage manager David, who lived next door to Etai but whom I hardly ever saw outside of rehearsal. Once I ran into him while he was wearing a helmet and holding a bike, just standing there not moving. David was the closest thing to an authority figure that we had, and seeing him in the blaring light of the real world was always jarring—like seeing a transvestite without her wig.

We waved to each other. Then I ran away down the street.

All in all, we were one big, Hunky family.

One night, early in the rehearsal process, fellow newbie Etai and I met for breakfast-for-dinner to get reacquainted. As luck would have it, we'd actually met before *Wicked*—in New York, working together on a musical my friend had written about a little girl dying of cancer. It was originally titled *The Chocolate Tree*, but I affectionately called it "The Cancer Musical" because I am just that classy. Etai, who was barely 5'6", had played a thirteen year-old and I, a member of the ensemble, had played a piranha, a jaunty French citizen, an astronaut, and others.

"So, you pronounce it 'e-TAI?' My mind is blown," I said as I gracefully licked Nutella off of the side of my palm. "All this time I'd been saying EEE-tai. Like 'meat-pie' where you stress the word 'meat.'"

"You're filthy," said Etai.

Etai said "filthy" around 100 times per conversation as a stand-in for any adjective, but somehow I always got his meaning. In this case, I think he meant *hilarious*.

Soon we got to talking about more pressing matters, like our hopes for what *Wicked* would be for us. It was familiar touchy-feely actor stuff, punctuated by the word "filthy" and Etai's constant shoulder-grabbing.

"So how are you liking rehearsals?" Etai asked.

"I like them as much as I like slowly slipping into the coils of insanity," I said.

"I think I know what you mean."

Rather than rehearse together, Etai and I had our own, entirely separate rehearsals, six days a week, at various dance studios scattered about the city. Each night we would return to the theater, drained from the hours of work, and spend the evening watching the show, either from the audience or from the wings, taking notes on the actors we would soon be replacing.

We gabbed a bit more, then ordered dessert (because after a Nutella crepe, this was the next logical step), at which point I declared that rehearsing for *Wicked* was exactly like Plato's Allegory of the Cave:

We were confined to learn about a civilization, chained in darkness, imagining the buildings, the people, the culture—hoping that, when we were finally set free, we would fit in, rather than be outcasts—stunted individuals out-of-step from reality, like Jodie Foster's leaf-eating, breast-baring character in that movie *Nell*.

"That's a filthy analogy," said Etai. "Just pure filth."

"But it's true, right?"

Dessert arrived, and we changed topics.

I soon learned that Etai had gone to school at the highly reputable University of Michigan where, unlike me, he'd completed a musical theater conservatory program.

"What's that like?" I asked, since I'd often wondered about this road not taken—the road of a Bachelor of Fine Arts. "Was it super intense?"

Etai explained that in a conservatory, an entire curriculum might be based on breathing, balance, or diction—the fundamentals of theater that every actor should take the time to learn.

I thought of my own college experience. By its own admission, Yale didn't really train you to *do* anything in particular. You "learned how to learn," or something like that. Which explained why, after completing my Frankensteinian English major—along with a hodge-podge of liberal arts courses (including "Language Abilities in Animals" and "Death")—the most I'd ever learned in the way of theater came from the workshops, occasional master classes, and student extracurriculars I did on top of my course load.

Etai described his senior showcase—the time when the theater majors put on a performance for industry casting directors and agents. This, he said, had been his most crucial foray into the theater business. Yale, in contrast, didn't do that sort of thing for undergrads.

"Then how did you get an agent?" Etai asked.

"I emailed her," I said, which was the truth. I'd compiled a video of my college theater performances and emailed the link to about 150 agents. Two replied; one of them was Ann. "It was a little luck, a little me-beating-the-system," I said.

I liked talking to Etai because he had a healthy perspective. He was immersed in theater but was able to speak critically of it. We touched upon some of my favorite topics—the quest to find an agent; the blood, sweat, and tears of auditioning; those "musical theater types" (people who say "fierce" or "belt your face" and talk about themselves loudly at auditions, hogging the airwaves to broadcast their personal life stories, wants, and dreams).

"I'm pretty sure those kinds of people think musical theater is about singing the highest and loudest note possible, and being able to *kick your face!*" Etai said.

"When did that become a thing," I asked, "like, that people encourage you to *do* things to your face? How is it even possible to 'belt' or 'kick' one's face?"

"Those people make me want to..."

Instead of finishing in words, Etai reached for my neck, as if to wring it, then rested his hands on my shoulders (where else?), shaking them to drive the point home.

"They're not interested in honoring character or story. It's just...filthy."

"Let's never be like that," I said, enjoying our time treading in this shared pool of agreement.

After finishing off a ginger cookie, I took a sip of water and said, out of the blue,

"Have you ever felt like you don't *entirely* belong?"

"What do you mean?"

"Like that you're an outsider. Like: that theater is what you do, but not necessarily all of who you are?"

As soon as I heard the words leave my mouth, I felt silly. But Etai looked pensive.

"Hm. I've definitely felt like the odd man out sometimes, in certain productions, and around certain groups of people. But doing theater is where I want to be. That's always been the case. And it's what I want to keep doing for the rest of my life."

"Yeah. Me too," I said.

I think?

As we paid the check, I beamed at Etai, my little crepe-eating companion.

I had found a friend. And a filthy one, at that.

9. LOOK, MA! I'M A PROFESSIONAL ACTOR!

"Eet weel be all right—I feex!" said Taisia, the Russian lady *Wicked* had assigned to be my dresser. "I weel have done by eight o'clock!" she called, bounding away to the costume room.

What she was going to feex was the clasp on my wool schoolgirl skirt, which, due to recent developments, would need to be moved about one quarter-inch for the remainder of the run. And by "recent developments," I mean stress eating like there was no tomorrow. Resizing seemed to be a trend, as several days prior I had to get a different headpiece for the opening, since the two hats they'd ordered in XL wouldn't fit my giant egg of a noggin. But, more disconcertingly, today I'd sized-out of some of my original costume measurements (specifically in the belly region) just in time for my first performance.

Further derailing matters, I'd arrived home last night to find a giant gift basket on my stoop, overflowing with cheese, crackers, and chocolate (the three major food groups), which I had no choice but to consume immediately.

The carb-sweet-fat basket was a surprise gift from my very own Gentle Rambo, one Marshall Roy who, even from 3,000 miles away, was crushing all of my ex-boyfriends' high scores. It was the latest of several culinary gestures from Mr. Roy—the first of which was a package filled with two dozen hand-baked oatmeal date cookies, which I devoured on the evening I received them. (I will win medals for stress eating when left to my living-alone-in-a-new-place devices.) Despite the unfortunate side effects, his special food deliveries were the most romantic things anyone had ever done for me, tied with the time in kindergarten when a boy named Harrison made me a picture book out of construction paper in which he declared his favorite color was white, his favorite movie was *The Little Mermaid*, and that he liked me very much.

Luckily, Taisia was a whiz at alterations, and, despite my worst efforts, it looked like everything was actually going to be okay.

Now, the only thing left was actually *doing* the damn show.

"This is half-hour, everyone, half-hour please. At tonight's performance, Fiama will be on as Madame Morrible, and Felicia will be making her Wicked *debut—welcome, Felicia. Thank you, everyone, half-hour."*

At 7:30 p.m. the voice over the intercom confirmed that this was all in fact real, and not another iteration of the dream I'd been having since childhood. The one where I start out as me—average, everyday gal, with questionable fashion sense—then suddenly get plucked from oblivion to perform onstage with various Broadway stars. In most dreams it's Douglas Sills from Broadway's *The Scarlet Pimpernel*, with whom (as you'll recall from my Dating History Museum) I was literally obsessed from the ages of 11 to 15. I even made a wall calendar for him, in which every month was a giant picture of his face, which I presented to him outside the Minskoff Theatre stage door. In dream world, we always played opposite each other, even though I was a pre-adolescent and he was pushing forty.

Nothing about this was creepy.

Tonight, I was sitting at my dressing room station amongst my new large-breasted companions, doing exactly as I'd been taught. I looked as I'd dreamed I might: my hair tightly matted under a black nylon wig cap and my face luminous with rouge, lip tint, and eyebrow pencil. It felt so good to be—or at least look, in all the measurable ways—completely prepared.

Like I *might* just belong.

"You ready, girl?" blonde-haired Alexa asked, as she slid her microphone pack down her back.

(All ensemble women wore their microphone packs low, in Velcro pouches at the back of *Wicked*-issued g-strings. They'd thread the cord up to their wig caps, coiling and tucking the wire underneath, while the little mic head stuck down onto their foreheads.)

"I think so," I said.

At fifteen minutes 'til curtain, I had been called onstage to practice my various dancer lifts—the *finale ultimo* to my weeks of grueling rehearsal. This was pretty standard, it turned out; every once in a while the dance captains would summon ensemble pairs to run the trickier routines, refreshing everyone's form and making sure everything was being done safely. After my potato-sack genital-assault on Patrick at my New York callback, I welcomed any dancer-lift practice with open, flailing arms.

Now, in the dressing room mirror, I was a sight to behold—flanked by the bouquets that had been sent to me by my parents, my Grandma, my agent, my Gentle Rambo. *Break a leg*, they said. *We're so proud of you.*

Everyone else thought it. Now it was time for me to embrace it: I was a cast member of *Wicked*.

Tonight was my first official night as one of the girls—without stage manager David or the dance captains as chaperones. I looked around me with wide-eyed wonder. I was the naïve freshman who'd finally been invited to eat lunch with the seniors. And they were all so...*cool*.

Each girl had her own effortless style. Penelope wore low-slung sweatpants, made extra-stylish by a cropped cotton tee that hung off her shoulders. Neka glided around in a short, black wrap. Alexa wore Ugg boots and a bathrobe she'd had the costume team tailor to her figure.

Me? I was clomping around in a standard-issued, white terry cloth robe, with cushiony blue hospital slippers that had my name Sharpied on them. In our fashion-show lineup, I was wearing Mom Jeans.

As I put the finishing touches onto my makeup, some girls did lunge-stretches on the ground, while others brushed their teeth or gargled in the sink. Each pre-show ritual was different, and most girls had no ritual at all. For them, preparing for a performance had as much ceremony as popping in a breath mint, or plucking one's eyebrows.

You ready, girl?

After hearing the five-minute announcement over the intercom, I filed out of the dressing room to the girls' changing gondola, where, with the help of our dressers, we donned our costumes for the Act I opening number (which for me was one outfit layered beneath another—preparation for a lightning-quick change that would happen six minutes into the show).

Taisia, my dresser, was fiddling with my snaps and zippers with darting fingers, muttering things in Russian each time she failed to press or loop something right on the first try. She was slightly new to the job, but it may as well have been her first day—such was the nature of working with a new cast member.

She and I would have to find our groove, our rhythm, our system, and it could take weeks.

"Over time, you would learn how to get everything on and off..."

I drifted back to the memory of trying on costumes in New York—the very costume I was being snapped into that night. Amanda had been right: some of my costume changes had been choreographed down to every last button and eyehook. I'd even watched Laura (the girl I replaced) many times backstage—to observe, take notes, and commit to memory not just everything she did while onstage but everything she did while *off*—from wig swaps, to makeup touch-ups, to when and how often it was advisable to pee.

Now it was my turn.

Dozens of snaps later, the intercom announced it was "places" and we, in our costumes-within-costumes, marched up the stairs to the main stage level like fat, multicolored ducks. Through the wings we made our way onstage, shielded from the audience by a map of the Land of Oz. There I saw the assistant stage manager Sue taking attendance, her permed hair looking particularly voluminous.

I weaved to the middle of the center clump—the first coordinates of my 3F track—like I'd done in rehearsal so many times before. Only this time, my imagination was made real—the characters and scenery popping out of my personal storybook.

And I was no longer alone.

"Ready, Frishé?" asked Penelope. I think she called me Frishé because it combined my first initial with my last name (F + Ricci = Frishé).

"Yes, I think so!" I said.

"Just have fun," said my shaved-headed neighbor Tim, giving me a camp-counselor pat on the back. "That's what this is all about!"

Thanks to Tim, I was reminded of all those years in summer theater camp, and all the student productions I'd done in high school and college. This would be just like those, right?

Except much, much bigger.

Here, the people surrounding me were the people I used to gaze at in awe on Broadway stages, or at the Providence Performing Arts Center where national tours would play. When I was a leg-swinging kid, heart fluttering from excitement, they all seemed years (even decades) older than I was—each impossibly gifted, gliding on air, at least twelve feet tall.

But here I was, among the *professionals*, grazing with them in their natural habitat. Moments before the show, they were all so relaxed, still themselves—laughing, joking, talking about last night's reality television. I was on a precipice, while everyone else was at their 9 to 5.

The pre-show announcement blared through the speakers, advising the audience not to take flash photography or unwrap crinkly candies. Then, in a sudden exclamation, the overture began. With a few moments to spare, the cast trickled down into their pre-show positions (where I had already been standing at attention, frozen like a statue).

I listened to the music, its melody propelling forward, and began my countdown.

3...2...1...

Look, Ma! I'm a professional actor!

Eleven scenes, eight costume changes, four rib-bruising lifts, two Red Bulls, and one curtain call later, I was an official cast member of *Wicked*.

Exhausted, I trudged up the stairs to the stage door. It was my first time greeting fans and lovers of *Wicked* while behind the velvet stanchion, as opposed to outside it.

I made this wall calendar for you, Mr. Sills!

A few fans holding souvenir programs nodded and smiled, and one even said,

"Great show!"

This gave me instant warm fuzzies.

I speed-dialed Marshall as I walked to catch a train home, dodging a man with a dead squirrel hat who was urinating in a potted plant.

"Hello!" said a familiar man-voice, groggy since it was 2 a.m. in New York.

"I did it," I said.

"Woooooo!" yelled Marshall, ever the Mayor of Enthusiasmville, even through exhaustion.

"I think I could get the hang of this professional-theater thing," I said.

"Of course you can! You're a superstar. And guess what?"

"What?"

"A week from now, I'll be picking you up at the stage door."

"That's so wild. Is this really happening?"

"Yes."

There was a pause.

"Still sure you want to do this?" asked Marshall.

"Yes. Definitely."

I told him to get the heck back to sleep already, but he insisted we chat at least a little longer. Squirrel Hat Man began his approach, but I didn't care: I was too happy to be freaked out.

"Seriously, though. My life is so—"

I didn't want to say it. It felt sacrilegious, like giving the finger to a priest, or not liking Oprah. But it was true:

"—perfect! I half-expect something terrible to happen to me."

Like for Squirrel Hat Man to steal my purse and pee in it. (I didn't say this second part out loud, though, since I didn't want to worry Marshall.)

"Nothing terrible is going to happen to you. Not while I'm there to help you."

"Deal," I said, feeling my stomach lurch.

Was it excitement? Was it fear?

Is there ever really a way to tell?

10. BACK TO THE FUTURE, OR NEW YORK CITY

Two things I underestimated about Marshall Roy:
1) The volume of his snoring.
2) The persistence of his snoring.

A week of living with him and I underestimated them no more.

But was I surprised?

From the giant bins of whey protein he carried with his massive gorilla hands into my tiny Mission District studio apartment, to the fact that any meal of his required two iterations (i.e. second lunch, second dinner), when Marshall did anything, it was go big or go home.

Snoring was no different.

"Commit to the bit," Marshall would say.

And I admired this about him. When Marshall Roy decided to do something, he never looked back. It might take him some time to decide, but once he did, he was in it to win it.

This tenet best applied, of course, to the latest (for lack of a better word) *bit* of all: our new and sudden cohabitation.

This was a bit to which we would both *commit!*

Twelve days after my ensemble debut, I awoke to the feeling of a massive hand resting lightly against my waist, and the stifled sound of Marshall's inhale and exhale—which had (praise the Lord) gotten at least slightly quieter, like the engine of a car that had driven a few blocks down the street.

In the night, we had tossed and turned together like self-preparing salads, never sleeping for more than a half-hour at a time. We reached relative equilibrium once Marshall discovered that flopping over onto his belly tamed the snoring beast within him. By that point, the sun had started to come up, but we'd power-napped for as long as possible.

Now, in the peace of the morning, our night of trauma seemed far behind, and I was the happiest I'd ever been. I'd conquered being in the ensemble of *Wicked*, and my brand-new boyfriend had come to stay.

Everything was in its right place. Sort of.

I looked around me.

We were as happy as little love-drunk clams, sharing a single cluttered shell overflowing with things, which we'd sometimes tidy, sometimes not. Our formula of folded clothes, unmade bed, and lowered toilet seat made us neat, but not *too* neat—a huge upgrade for me. Before Marshall arrived, I'd been flinging my goods around with the unbridled creativity of an artist (which is my way of saying I'd been a slob). But in the five days since Marshall's arrival, I'd managed to sweep and stack most things into little compartments here and there, making room for a giant gladiator in my one-room studio.

With my index finger I poked Marshall's bicep, which was peeking out from his white Hanes t-shirt. He stirred and rolled his arm back over his head, offering me his armpit. I burrowed in, sniffing his Old Spice musk. You're going to gag but, honestly, there was no smell I loved more than Marshall's armpits. (I once told him that if I ever wore his deodorant, I would likely be attracted to myself.)

After a few moments of armpit sniffing, I began my morning ritual of unfurling slowly into waking life, like a flower to the light—except much less gracefully, and with a huge, visible wedgie.

"Where you going, little friend?" Marshall rumbled as I untangled my last limb from the swirl of white bed sheets.

"Gotta pee," I squealed, running away, trying to de-wedgie myself. "Plug your ears!"

On this—a Wednesday—we would have all morning together. The working plan was to enjoy a late brunch at Boogaloos, a killer breakfast spot precisely one block from the Hunky House. Then I would be due downtown for *Wicked*'s matinee.

"What time do you have rehearsal today?" Marshall called through the flimsy bathroom doors, which weren't so much doors as suggestions that maybe you shouldn't come in.

I gripped the tiny hook knobs, trying to pull them further together to seal the two flimsy panels—a room divider between me and humiliation.

"I told you, I cannot talk to you while I pee!" I shouted.

Marshall had arrived late on a Saturday night and met me at the stage door, suitcase in tow, his smile big as ever. He'd scooped me up in his arms, at which point I let him kiss my sweaty face and recently un-pin-curled hair, which had been doused in the salty goodness that was my abundant sweat. No-holds-barred unkemptness in front of Marshall was a first for me, since during our courtship I'd upheld the illusion that I was put-together, well-groomed, and effortlessly poised. (Sort of.)

A mere three months in, and I suddenly had to face a girl's worst fear: showing herself as she was. Without makeup, primping, or the distancing formality of a dinner date. He would have to take me as I was. And vice versa.

I swung open the wood panels and promenaded into the bedroom to see Marshall lying diagonally across the bed, clicking through his cell phone.

"Weather.com says that every day this week it's going to be cloudy and 60 degrees."

"Oh, sorry about that," I said.

"No, I wasn't complaining. In New York it's, like, 12 degrees."

"Ah. But don't get too excited. Weather here is a fickle mistress."

Marshall lay his phone down on the end table, next to my own. "Cell phone friends," we called them, in our sickening love haze. He stretched his arms over his head while I lowered down onto the bed, watching him. His face was stubbly, and his eyelids were still at half-mast. He looked like a groggy newborn. But sexy. Like, a sexy, groggy newborn.

"I like that I get to see you like this," I said.

"Oh, now I'm embarrassed," said Marshall, hiding his head under the covers.

"Come on. You saw me pluck my eyebrows yesterday and pop a zit on my chin."

"But you looked really good when you did that," said Marshall, wrangling for my stomach. I screamed as he bound his hands around my waist and scooped me to him, pulling me back into the bedsheets from which I had worked so hard to escape.

I pleaded. "Marsh! My call time is one-thirty!"

Since it was Wednesday, I was due at the theater for the afternoon matinee, followed by an evening performance. It sounds like a lot, but I'd grown accustomed to having my days and nights full. Since my ensemble debut, I was rehearsing the part of Elphaba during the day, and performing at night. Two-show days Wednesday and Saturday were, ironically, my only respite.

"Okay, I'm getting up," Marshall rumbled as he finally planted one long, muscular leg onto the carpet.

"You're such a hottie," I swooned, acting the damsel to my knight in shining Hanes.

While walking by, Marshall patted the side of my bum—his wordless reply. Then, from inside the bathroom, he called,

"Speaking of hot, which way do I turn on the faucet again?"

"To the left!" I yelled. "Remember, it's counterintuitive!"

Our freestanding bathtub-slash-shower was an ancient marvel, possibly from the Elizabethan Era. You know, the kind that have legs and look like fat porcelain pets that might up and walk away one day. It was barely large enough for a toddler, and was surrounded by a wraparound curtain that clung to you with cold, slimy determination. The showerhead itself was an insult to indoor plumbing everywhere, raining pitiable spurts of water, like warm, begrudging spit. I strained to listen for Marshall slinking his way in, gasping from the cold sheen of the curtain, and imagined how he must look—cramped and corralled, the only adult in the kiddie pool.

As I approached our shared dresser, I glanced at my cell phone and saw the white light flashing, indicating a voicemail. While hoisting on my easy jeans and button-down, I listened over the speaker.

"Hi, Felicia—"

I'd know that Southern braying anywhere!

"—it's Ann. Give me a call when you get this."

Click!

Oh, Ann. My agent. Ever the charmer. No matter how terse the message, I smiled at the thought that she was calling to check up on me, her new client on her first big show.

"Who was that, Fel?" asked Marshall, stepping from the bathroom. He'd wrapped a towel around his waist, and water droplets glistened on his pectorals.

"My agent. I'll give her a call on the way."

The Hunky House was perched on the steepest hill I'd ever seen. It was less like a hill and more like a step-less staircase, or just, like, an elevator shaft you had to climb down. On our way to brunch, Marshall volunteered to carry me, but I desperately needed the workout.

In minutes we reached Boogaloos, recurring site of my many breakfast bonanzas. Before entering, I dialed Ann on my cell.

"Hello!" she yelled.

Oh, how I have missed the decisively unpleasant though well-meaning sound of her voice!

"Ann! Hi! I'm, uh, just returning your call!"

"So, I take it you're ready for your trip?" Ann replied.

Was that a metaphor? As was my custom when translating Annglish, I held for clarification. But there was only silence.

"Ha ha," I said. "What do you mean?"

"Your trip tomorrow. To New York. Or is this news to you?"

My eyes must have been bugging out, because I saw Marshall mouthing,

What's wrong?

I'm not sure, I mouthed back, following up to Ann in actual words,

"Is everything okay?"

"Well, pack your sack and come home to Mama! 'Cause you've got another audition to get to."

"Really? For what?"

"For *Wicked!*"

"Um..."

Was Ann in her right mind?

"I'm already *in Wicked*," I said, wondering if this was less a real scene from my life than a prank reality show, or a Marx Brothers' bit disguised as a conversation.

Ann cackled.

"Darling, no. You're getting another shot! They want to audition you to be the new Elphaba standby."

More bug-eyes. Marshall's face morphed into an actual question mark.

"Oh, wow!" I said, mouthing, *I have to fly to New York*. Then, to Ann, "And this is all happening tomorrow?"

"Yep. Same packet as your audition and callback. Do you need me to re-send the materials?"

"Nope, I've got them," I said, patting my catchall tote, inside which I'd placed my Elphaba binder. I brought it with me everywhere, since I'd been studying my lines and music on the train and during my ensemble performances.

News of the audition felt like I was suddenly getting thrust into the future—where I would be held accountable for my Elphaba work so far. At the same time, it was like a journey into the past—back to New York, where it had all started.

In both scenarios, I was being tested. Again.

And I was woefully unprepared.

(**GREEN. 5.** not fully developed or perfected in growth or condition; unripe; not properly aged: *a green actress*.)

"You need to figure out flights with management. Talk to...what's his name? Tanaka?"

"Sure, I will."

"Well, away we go—right, darling?"

❖ ❖ ❖

"Tanaka" was Annglish for Tanase, *Wicked* San Francisco's company manager. He was the local liaison to the *Wicked* Powers-That-Be, the committee of fates that was apparently orchestrating my next cross-continental adventure.

Who were these mysterious fates?

I wondered if Tanase dealt with them on a regular basis, what with their long beards, bauble staffs, and elixir-filled chalices. (That's how I pictured them, anyway.) How did the lot of them communicate? Telepathy? Smoke signals? Skype?

The weirdest part about these fates? If it were up to me, I'd never have cast myself, let alone invited me to re-audition. As I shook from nerves, I realized that they had more faith in me than I ever could.

Seriously. What were they thinking?

I knocked on Tanase's door, craning in to see him sitting at his desk, unflinching. He waved his hand for me to come in. Tanase was much younger than I expected a company manager to be, with clean good looks and a manicured sheen that would make Tim Gunn proud. While always helpful, Tanase gave the distinct impression that his mind orbited his mouth: as he spoke about one thing, he collected far-out idea-bits and thought-satellites in the stratosphere. Maybe it was all in my imagination, but I got the distinct impression that sometimes he was actually on an international space station, way out on a neighboring planet, while his body operated remotely. (Maybe Neptune. Or Uranus.) The Tanase who sat at his desk was a surrogate; the real Tanase was doing something more important for mankind.

I crept onto the thin blue carpet, and we started chatting about my trip.

"Here are some flight options," Tanase said. "You would be excused from Thursday and Friday's performances, then due back for the matinee Saturday."

Leaning over his shoulder to see the computer, I decided on a flight that would leave the next evening and return Friday, which meant I would stay in New York City overnight. Since I had sublet my Hell's Kitchen apartment, *Wicked* would be housing me at the

Mayfair Hotel, a happy six blocks from where the audition would take place.

As Tanase typed, I looked around. His desk was immaculate, with neatly arranged penholders and a few framed photos of him wearing zipper sweaters in front of strange mountainscapes. (Was that Uranus? I wondered.) If *Wicked*'s theater contained a tug-of-war between fantasy and reality, the company management office was the epicenter of reality—the perfect contrast to what went on onstage.

Outside was Oz. In here were forms, logistics, rules, and practicalities.

"So, looks like we're all set," said Tanase's mouth, while his mind was steering him through an intergalactic hailstorm. "I'll bring you the confirmation details by tonight's performance. And be sure to save your receipts—checked baggage, taxi from the airport, that sort of thing."

I thanked him, then darted out of the room to try to find Bryan, the conductor and music director. I'd crammed for tons of tests in college—learning a semester's worth of material in the final hours—and this standby audition would be no different.

Not if I had anything to do with it.

Bryan was like a distant, power-suit-wearing father. No matter how much he scared me, I just wanted him to love me. And then come to my soccer game.

At 6:30 p.m. I swung by the vocal rehearsal room, whose door was propped open, and caught Bryan sitting on the miniature couch, eating a dinner of what looked like falafel and French fries.

"Come in!" he said, not looking up—even though I was already in the room, at which point I considered walking out then coming back in, so as not to upset him.

Instead, I boldly took to the center of the room, a mere foot from where he was sitting, and set my binder on the music stand.

"Thanks for coaching me," I said, as Bryan glided over to the piano bench.

Without a moment to spare, he started to play the familiar vamp of rolling chords—the ones I'd heard at my audition, my callback, then every night through the dressing room monitors, over which Teal Wicks, our Elphaba, would sing:

"Unlimited..."

"STOP!" Bryan spun around on the bench to face me. He frowned at me like I had mustard, or boils, on my face. "You weren't thinking, were you?"

"Uh—" I shook my head and shrugged.

"What were you thinking?"

I am so scared of you, that is what I was thinking.

"Uh, I guess," I stalled, "I was focusing on my notes and breathing, just trying to focus, for now."

"Yes, I could tell. I know because you *inhaled* way too early."

At this he closed his eyes and looked down, pausing before an open casket—showing due respect for the death of talent and reason.

"Your breath should come *with* the sound, directly before you phonate. If you're present, this happens naturally. If not, your breathing is totally off."

"Oh, okay. Right. Thank you," I said, wondering if he'd learned this subtle giveaway in the guidebook of *Evil Music Director Detectivery.*

"Again!"

Rolling cords. Steeled mind.

Think of something, anything!

"Unlimited..."

"STOP!"

Motherfu—

"What were you thinking?" said Bryan, this time not even turning to face me. Without waiting for me to answer, he asked, "What does it mean to see that something is 'unlimited'?"

I furrowed my brow.

"Uh..."

Unlimited. What did a word that was so unspecific mean to Elphaba, specifically?

I was learning the hard way that singing wasn't just breath, posture, or vowel placement; singing was *acting*. And acting wasn't black turtlenecks and berets—acting was *specificity*. *Specificity* was the imagination, channeled concretely. Imagination was risky, because it involved decision-making, deciding what a character—a person—might think, feel, believe, experience.

I took a deep breath, closed my eyes, and inched onto the ledge of my imagination.

Time to take a risk.

"Elphaba sees, uh, a giant statue of herself. With people all around, cheering. That's the celebration that's 'all to do with her.' You know? That's what she's singing about."

I held my breath.

Bryan cocked his head to the side and, this time, spun around to look me in the face.

"Really? Is that *really* how Elphaba sees her future? As a giant statue?"

"Well, no." Clearly I'd failed the quiz. This was *hard*.

Then, I thought: I couldn't think about Elphaba as some abstract, green alien. I needed to think of myself first. And ask, "What would *I* want?"

What is an unlimited future?

Not bound by conventional strictures, by the shackles that have always held me back.

I closed my eyes. The lyrics mentioned that all of Oz would be celebrating something about Elphaba. Everyone, together.

"We're holding hands," I said.

"Who?"

"A huge circle of people. Hundreds of people. Outside. In a field."

"What else?" coaxed Bryan.

"We're all...green."

"Better," said Bryan. "Let's take it again."

I took a breath.

As I began my pin curls that evening before the performance, I wondered why I'd been given this second opportunity. What did the long-bearded *Wicked* fates see in me? Was it timing? Was it convenient? Was it that they wouldn't have to pay me much? Or had I, in just a week of rehearsal, made a good enough impression that others saw in me something that I couldn't see in myself?

Or was it that I was so similar to Elphaba—a near-match for the hotheaded green protagonist?

I didn't know whether to be flattered, or offended.

One by one the rest of the ensemble girls trickled in, greeting me and each other. It occurred to me that over the past month I'd become part of something great: a member of *Wicked*'s ensemble. One of the gang—a group of friends.

If I got promoted to standby, I wondered, would that change everything? In a sense, all this ensemble work would have been for nothing, and I would have to defect from the community— going it alone once again, an apparent theme in my social life.

Maybe Libby, the new Glinda standby, would be my compatriot?

As if on cue, the door swung open and in flounced Libby, wearing a strapless dress patterned with a bunch of mini pink dogs—a textile that must have been woven on Barbie's dream loom.

"Hey, everyone!" she sang, arabesquing her way to the far wall of dressing room mirrors, chatting with a gaggle of girls. In moments, she was standing behind me, beaming into my mirror with unjustifiable glee.

"So, how was your first week?" she squealed.

I half-expected her to start French braiding my hair or playing Patty Cake with the side of my face.

"It was great!" I said. "What about you? Is your put-in next Friday?"

"Yes, I think so. It's been nice having Glinda rehearsal since playing it on tour."

"Totally."

I considered bringing up the fact that I was about to fly to New York to audition to be Elphaba standby, but I felt weirdly nervous mentioning it.

We chatted a bit more about where the two of us were living, our favorite restaurants, our hometowns—that sort of thing.

"Well, break a leg," I finally said, in that way you do when a conversation is about to be over. (My giddiness hourglass had all but emptied to its last small-talk grain.)

"Byeeee!" said Libby, practically pirouetting out the door.

This could be my future, I thought.

Help.

❖ ❖ ❖

Ninth Avenue was familiar but strange, a ghost city resurrected from a past life. That Thursday evening, I stalked along the sidewalk, bleary-eyed from the six-hour flight, past my old apartment. It was odd to be so close to home, yet unable to return there—like I'd come back as a different person.

I ducked into a restaurant for a solo dinner of spaghetti, searching for comfort in carbohydrates. As I was finishing, I gave best friend Becky a call.

"Hey, son!"

"Son! I am in New York!"

"I cannot believe I am out of town! Are you okay?"

"I'm fine, just kind of wandering. My audition is early tomorrow. I just met with my pianist friend Zak at a studio, and we ran the Elphaba songs. Then I bought a pair of really expensive boots."

"That is amazing! Why did you do that?"

I told Becky about how our current Elphaba standby, for whose spot I was auditioning (since she had been promoted to Elphaba on one of the tours), had late last night advised me to put extra effort into selecting appropriate footwear. She had explained that high heels were off the character-mark, whereas strong, sturdy boots would be best.

"Be sure to look long and lean!" she'd admonished, as if this could be accomplished with a shoe.

Even if the advice sounded silly, as an overachiever cramming for the exam I would take any and all advice in stride. (Literally.) So sturdy boots it was.

"So I have these new shoes for maybe no reason. Now I just hope I can, like, hit the notes."

"Son, it's in the bag. Just do your thing," said Becky.

We chatted some more as I detoured into a corner deli, picking up three giant bottles of water, a packet of spearmint gum and, of course, a banana.

That night, I couldn't sleep, but could only hear, rolling in my head, over and over,

"Unlimited..."

At the audition the next morning, I strode through a foreign land, conspicuously lacking the seizure-inducing green wall and Un-Funhouse doors. After consulting a digital board, I found my way to the assigned studio.

Not having slept a wink, I was running on adrenaline, nervous fumes, and the starchy potassium-filled bulk of one banana, consumed an hour before my 11:20 a.m. appointment. Through the perception-bending door I heard, of course, someone singing "Defying Gravity" absolutely perfectly. I closed my eyes, tightly, as if this would shut out the sound.

In doing so, I felt a dreadful wave of exhaustion. From my sleepless nights with Marshall to my flight to New York, the count of hours I'd gone without rest had begun to rise—like a dangerous riptide.

Last night the Mayfair Hotel had made the Hotel Whitcomb look like a French chateau. My room had been so cramped that its walls could have been the bed's four posters. The mattress felt like a slab of rock, while every object in the room—from the wallpaper, to the bedspread, to the window treatment—was patterned in a blue print of a man hunched over a sheep, holding a shepherd's staff and a rope. This was either meant to be pastoral, or taboo erotica.

I opened my eyes, hitting my hand against the side of my face. Just then, the door opened and out walked a lithe, black-haired, eerily familiar girl. At first I thought that the strains of sleep deprivation would make anyone look eerie, if not familiar.

Then it hit me.

Edvard Munch!

She was one of the two girls from my dance callback—the one who'd been as horrible at dancing as I was!

We looked at each other and exchanged stiff smiles.

Soon the door swung open with a frightful clap, and casting director Craig appeared (as was his habit) telling Edvard Munch she was free to go—which meant I was next.

Hadn't I been here, twice before? The déjà vu was back, but this time it was the dream-sequence version. The air felt gluey; the light was hazy.

Inside the audition room, I saw Paul-Alan-Nick, whose real name was Paul, with his searing blue eyes; along with Lombardo, whose name, it turned out, was Dominick; along with some others, many of whom had actually come to San Francisco to visit the cast and hold rehearsals over the past few weeks. *Wicked* was a huge operation, so the New York creative team, including the people who sat before me, would occasionally beam down to Broadway's various satellite companies (like San Francisco) to make sure all was in working order. Then they'd beam back to the mothership.

Today, I'd been invited aboard, for a brief and privileged hearing.

A woman named Lisa sat in the center, with a furrowed brow and unruly curls the color of sand. She was the associate director, and spoke first.

"I like your shoes," she said.

"Oh, thanks," I said.

Booyah!

I glanced down at my army green wedge-heeled Stuart Weitzmans, smiling like I'd just given birth to them, adding,

"They're industrial, and yet feminine."

(Exorbitant callback boots: priceless.)

"Let's start with 'The Wizard and I,'" said Lisa.

I nodded to the pianist, who began those infamous rolling chords.

Be specific!

As I prepared to sing, through my sleep deprivation I noted that if there were a movie version of my *Wicked* experience, it would absolutely include three or more slow-motion montages set to this confounded music. Meanwhile, I'd be riding horseback on the beach in a white flowy dress, alongside Richard Gere, who would be brushing strands of hair from my face. Because that's what happens in movie montages.

Okay, focus!

The room had flooded with sound.

We're holding hands. And we're all...green.

11. NOW WHAT?

And thus began seven days of waiting—also known as the Week I Didn't Poop.

Back in San Francisco, I was hard-pressed to take my mind off of the audition. Something about the high drama of the ordeal—being whisked away on a plane, not sleeping, re-auditioning, but maybe dreaming it all—made me so tense that my bowels had become completely paralyzed. Not even guitar man or mattress lady—amidst other chaotic, crazy-person displays on the streets—could startle my intestines into working order.

(TMI—I know. But remember what I said about it being a memoir?)

"You can't let your nerves get the best of you," cautioned Marshall, as we lay awake in bed. "I think you might be putting too much pressure on yourself."

"You think?" I snapped back. It was 3 a.m., and tonight's tossing-and-turning match had reached epic, WWF proportions. We'd reached a temporary truce, but genuine shuteye was still far off. I lay flopped on my back, my legs and arms jutting out like a bug that had been squashed while doing a jumping jack.

"I'm sorry," I finally said, huffing and puffing through an exhale of an apology.

"It's okay, Fel," Marshall said, massaging his temples. "You just need to think about this whole standby thing as a win-win."

He propped himself up on one elbow. I could see in his face that he was about to give me advice, and I was too exhausted to object.

"Here's the thing," he began.

I leaned in on my elbows to listen.

In addition to "committing to the bit," Marshall was one of the most rational people I'd ever met, and that night I caught my first glimpse of him in action. With an unwavering can-do attitude, Marshall could break down any high-pressure situation into simple steps—like an Ikea manual for life.

"If you get the job, that's awesome," he said. "You'll be getting a promotion, and you'll be first in line to play your dream role. If you don't get it, you're where you were before this whole ordeal: performing in an amazing musical. There is no way to lose."

Marshall's rational assessment stirred me. I turned on my left side to face him.

"I see what you mean," I said, biting my lip. "But still...I guess...I just don't want to fail."

As soon as the words came out, my face got hot. I had never admitted out loud how potent my fear was.

I am afraid of failing.

So much so that my body was refusing to let me poop.

(Okay, if you're so squeamish about natural human functions, just skip to the end of the chapter.)

"You're so hard on yourself," Marshall said. "Failure is an event, not a state of being. It doesn't mean anything. Why are you so afraid of it?"

"I don't know," I said.

Had I, throughout my life, been collecting achievement chips, as a kind of currency for self-worth? If so, I hadn't realized it until now. But it all made sense: I was a classic overachiever, who'd crammed her way into an Ivy League school, then set her sights on success or bust. Had professional theater become the next frontier?

When it came to *Wicked*, I'd never been tested so many times or through such extremes, and the process had begun to take a toll. My old, horseshoe-wielding friend Luck wouldn't lay off the aggressive spankings. In my mind, this meant certain, spectacular failure.

Is that how achievement worked? That the more you accomplished, the worse you felt? That the higher you soared, the longer and farther you could fall as soon as the letdown arrived?

I peered into Marshall's face, his thick mass of eyelashes complementing his strong, Superman-like jaw. I was afraid of professional failure—but was I also confusing it with another fear?

They don't call it "falling" in love for nothing.

We talked through the night. Marshall's words helped, but I still couldn't shake the feeling of dread. How much further would I have to go—traveling down this long, winding, yellow brick road? Would I lose myself amidst so many challenges?

I had no choice but to press on, through the sleepless, poopless week.

❖   ❖   ❖

The days after my standby audition could also have been called, How Am I Anxious About Getting a Role that I Am Simultaneously Rehearsing? Because maybe the weirdest part was that in the aftermath, I had to continue on with my daily Elphaba rehearsals, while everyone on staff agreed to act like nothing had happened.

No dramatic cross-country flight. Nope. Business as usual.

Like my ensemble rehearsals, Elphaba rehearsals were split between blocking and vocals. The main difference between this and learning my ensemble track was that the Elphaba material was approximately one billion times scarier.

My most basic gripe was with all of the high belting. It was simply relentless—one song after the other, throughout the entire show. If potato-sack lifts had tested the limits of what I could do with my body, Elphaba was its vocal and mental equivalent.

Anyone who wanted to play Elphaba, I thought, had to be (on some level) deeply masochistic.

I was making almost undetectable progress on the singing, struggling everyday to find the confidence to say, "Yes, I can do this."

Because—honestly—I didn't know if I could.

And I wouldn't really know until I was onstage performing.

Like my part in the ensemble, Elphaba's every moment had been assigned a precise location. Since I wasn't creating the part from scratch, I wasn't coming up with the blocking myself. Instead I inherited the work of Idina Menzel (the original Elphaba), whose blocking had been passed down a long line of successors. Kristen the dance captain led me through Elphaba's songs, while stage manager David gave me the blocking.

Nothing was a suggestion—together they mapped out Elphaba's every move along the stage's grid coordinates, telling me when to turn, where, and by how many feet.

To me, strict numbers made sense when it came to group dances. After all, it was important to maintain formation, and for songs and scenes to have a cohesive, choreographed precision.

But when it came to scene work—actual speak-your-lines-on-this-mark as Elphaba—I felt a tangle of marionette strings pulling me in all directions.

Meanwhile, stage manager David would speak every other character's lines in a stirring monotone while I chased my tail around the stage, poring over my note-scribbled binder like a lost hunchback. I recited the lines as I thought I was supposed to, in a voice that seemed partly my own, partly a chorus of synthesized strains from the Elphabas who'd come before me—whom I'd studied here in San Francisco, on Broadway, or on YouTube.

They were all speaking in unison, while I lip-synced through each rehearsal.

And, ohmygod I just want to poop.

"So, regardless of how things, uh, *turn out,*" David said during one of our ten-minute breaks, "we'll stick to the same Elphaba schedule for you."

My ears perked up. I smelled intrigue.

How things turn out?

"Sounds good," I said, wanting to be like,

JUST TELL ME, DAMMIT, FOR THE LOVE OF ALL THAT IS GOOD!

David's eyes darted down to his binder as he hummed, softly.

Just when I thought I couldn't take it any longer, and that my bowels would have to be submitted for urgent medical care, I got word later that afternoon.

If I was destined to "fail," it wouldn't be that day. Nope. I could breathe a sigh of relief—for now.

For now, I was the new Elphaba standby.

I promptly took the longest, most satisfying dump of my life.

12. SONGS OF DEATH,
OR, MEET EDEN ESPINOSA

The *Wicked* casting twister was unstoppable. Soon it had steered toward Teal Wicks, who played her final Elphaba performance at the end of February. As her replacement, the legendary Eden Espinosa dropped in, with the force of a house—the latest miraculous occurrence here in the Land of Oz.

Even at her young age, Eden had become a household name: originating the title role in *BKLYN: The Musical*, closing *Rent*'s run as Maureen, and being Idina Menzel's original Elphaba standby and the third actress ever to play the role on Broadway. A few years later, Eden had opened *Wicked*'s Los Angeles company, and now was back in San Francisco for another pass at being green. Fans and critics agreed: Eden was electrifying—her Elphaba reimagined with unmistakable strength and heart.

As her soon-to-be standby, I had big shoes to fill. With only a couple of weeks left before my put-in, I had to make a serious push to get my voice in shape. This would mean coming to grips with the challenges before me—namely, that three of Elphaba's nine songs gave me nightmares. These I called the "Songs of Death."

What were these Songs of Death? In chronological order:

1) "The Wizard and I"

2) "Defying Gravity"

3) "No Good Deed"

Alternate titles:

1) "Let's Put a Really High Song in Elphaba's First Scene"

2) "This Isn't a Joke, You Are Actually Expected to Sing This High While Flying"

3) "Let's Belt Some More and Run Around the Stage, Because Why Not"

Yes, the Songs of Death were—well? The songs that made me feel like I might keel over while singing them. The doozies. The destructors. The devils. I couldn't speak for other Elphabas, but for me these explosive, spew-your-guts Songs of Death demanded that every atom of my body spin around its individual nucleus in special, anxiety-driven hyper-speed. What's more, they were spaced evenly throughout the show, beginning when Elphaba first took the stage, punctuating the end of Act I, then reemerging at the eleventh hour, when all hope (and energy) had been lost. For these reasons, conquering the Songs of Death would never be quick and painless, but rather slow and agonizing—the difference between ripping off a Band-Aid and plucking every body hair, one at a time.

As Elphaba, your first song is "The Wizard and I." You perform this mere minutes after entering. Be cautioned: it's important to start strong. If you falter (your voice wobbles, or you crack) it can undermine your confidence for the rest of the show.

If you make it, you're in the clear until "Defying Gravity"—the most intimidating Song of Death. It falls at the end of Act I. Onstage during its climax, Elphaba must lift off into flight—a stirring declaration of strength and independence—while *belting her face* for the masses.

Leading up to this climax, you must place your prop broom in your left hand, use your right to unclasp your satchel and shake it to the floor, while crossing upstage, turning around, and gearing up for takeoff. Then, as you lift, you've got to bring out the vocal big guns: singing the highest (some might even say most torturous) collection of notes ever written—made that much worse because you have to belt them *as* you fly, high above the stage, waving your broom around in the air. This you do for a solid minute-and-a-half, ending the act with three sustained, vocal cord-splitting cries (*"Bring maaaa naaaa!"*).

Finally, there's "No Good Deed." Having been onstage for nearly two hours you have all but emptied your energy stores. But exhaustion be damned! Right before "No Good Deed" you must run (literally) offstage, down the backstage stairs, and through the orchestra pit, while wearing a thirty-odd pound dress and unpinning the back of your hair. Once in the pit, you must situate yourself inside a trap door elevator, which lifts you up through the floor in time for you to start singing. (And by "singing," I mean letting out a primal "Fiyerooooooo!" scream at the top of your throbbing lungs.) After that, you essentially just keep running around, throwing your body in all different directions while you sing really high, conveying the ultra-intense emotionality of the song.

Sound fun?

In the weeks before my put-in, when I wasn't rehearsing with conductor Bryan or *Where's Waldo* Steve I was practicing on my own. I did this in the shower, in my living room, or in a dusty rehearsal studio I'd been renting by the hour.

After screaming at the top of my lungs then collapsing onto the floor, I would often wonder, What would Eden Espinosa do? She'd performed as Elphaba for years. On the YouTube circuit alone she'd become a celebrity, with some performance clips garnering over 100,000 views. Clearly she was doing *something* right. Performing beside her each night in my ensemble track, I would watch her closely. To me, it was a mixture of spontaneity and genuineness that made her Elphaba irresistible.

Did it come naturally to her? Or had she faced all the challenges I was facing?

Practicing on my own, when I envisioned Eden in those dark, dusty moments, she seemed to hover on a higher plane. Maybe one day, I thought, I'd get to ask her all my questions—all that I'd been pondering during this strange and inexplicable journey.

I yearned now more than ever for her wisdom, and often daydreamed about getting to know her. Maybe being her standby meant I could become her loyal protégé, kissing her ring while she patted my head and spoke in profound, moralistic riddles. We'd lounge in togas on large rocks, eating grapes, engaging in philosophical dialogue. "What *is* art?" I would say, and Eden would respond in song, while nearby a young boy played a flute.

Or, at the very least, we could hang out or something.

This wasn't too far-fetched. I'd already met Eden once backstage, and before that had stalked her in a Starbucks. I spotted her getting coffee across from the Orpheum, and proceeded to watch my massive boyfriend accidentally run into her with his chair as he tried to claim a table (remember what I said about him being like Disney's teenage Hercules?). After that, we sat in the back and stared at Eden until she left.

Nothing about this was creepy.

Whatever the case, it was comforting to fast-forward to the day when I might get to know Eden, and absorb her vast stores of ancient performer wisdom. By then, all my trials would be behind me. And, like her, I would be able to confidently say, "I am Elphaba Thropp."

A week later and I got my first (exceedingly awkward) chance.

❖   ❖   ❖

"Okay, Catchphrase time!" announced Annie.

It was game night at Glinda standby Libby's apartment, a tradition newly forged by a small and dorktastic group of *Wicked* cast members. On these special Sundays we rang in the end of our eight-show week with rousing games of Catchphrase, Scattergories, and Charades, all while watching the MSNBC show *To Catch a Predator.*

"Someone would please explain the rules?" said Nic, who played Fiyero (*Wicked*'s romantic lead). He wore wide-rimmed glasses and a t-shirt with a picture of an electric guitar. "How is this game played, please?"

"Awww, Nic," said Libby.

Nic, who was French Canadian, hid his slight accent onstage, but sometimes let his foreignness creep into everyday conversation, at which point one or more of us would coo at him like he was a toddler speaking his first sentence.

"It's like that game Password, except with teams," began first-violinist Cary, our resident expert on everything.

As Cary explained the rules, Marshall seized the remote and started flipping through to find MSNBC. Nobody really understood why watching pedophiles get publicly shamed was part of our tradition; it just happened that the first time we'd assembled we'd gotten a huge kick out of it. Somehow, it stuck.

"Oh, look! There it is," said Libby, pointing to the TV and giggling.

On the screen there was a man in acid-wash jeans, who was later identified as a pastor, sitting on a stool by a kitchen counter. "What's in the bag?" asked host Chris Hansen in the most serious voice I'd ever heard. "Condoms?"

"No," said the pastor. Then he hung his head. "Yes."

"See? They're damned if they do, damned if they don't," said Etai, stirringly.

We all gasped as we watched the pastor get tackled to the lawn by a bunch of policemen with bowl haircuts.

"It's just pure filth," heckled Etai from his corner armchair.

"Are we ready to play?" called Annie, her smiley face at its smiliest.

"Hang on," Libby said, rising to her feet. In her frilly cardigan and sparkly headband she began lighting a row of tea lights, which she set next to the snack bowls and cheap wine Marshall and I had brought. From the looks of everything, Libby had cleaned and tidied her decidedly chic apartment. High-ceilinged and fully-furnished, it was part of a corporate housing building where many *Wicked* cast members lived.

"Libby, you are quite the hostess," I said as she walked over to the kitchen and grabbed a bowl of grapes.

"Oh, stop!" she said so cutely that I wanted to call the cute police.

"Need any help?" I asked.

"Just sit your pretty booty down," she said.

Lately, Libby and I had grown closer. Each game night we'd been swapping stories, testing our favored styles of conversation and senses of humor. Like Etai, Libby had gone to a conservatory program for college. Before that, she'd done summer theater— something we had in common—where she was hailed as an adorable little ingénue. (In contrast, I had tackled such roles as Fagin in *Oliver!*, Mercutio in *Romeo and Juliet*, Captain Hook in *Peter Pan*, and Fred Phelps and other men in *The Laramie Project*. Do you see a pattern? I was a gender-bending, feminist pioneer. With low self-esteem and bad acne.)

Indeed, Libby and I were a curious pair, on the honeymoon of our arranged standby marriage. We were eager to make things work, and in no time at all, the effort became minimal. Lately, it was no effort at all. I concluded that during my early days in the ensemble I had been quick to judge her; she was, despite her bubbly sheen, a kindred spirit. (I hope the obvious Glinda/Elphaba parallel comes to mind. No need for me to mention it, right? Oh, oops, I just did.)

"Okay, I think we're ready," said Cary, as Nic nodded while looking perplexed.

But we were interrupted as somebody outside started knocking. Libby answered and, in seconds, through the door walked—gasp!—Edvard Munch.

(Remember her?)

"Hey friends," she said, giving a little wave.

As of a week ago, Edvard Munch had become *Wicked*'s newest cast member. Since the Week I Didn't Poop, she'd been flown in as my ensemble replacement, and was now training to understudy Elphaba and perform my old 3F track.

I dug my hand into a bowl of Pirate's Booty as I glanced over at Edvard, who plopped down next to Etai. Her hair was long and tied low in a ponytail, her perfect cheekbones an art lesson in shadow and light.

"Alyssa, you're just in time," said Libby.

Yes, Edvard's real name was Alyssa, but I wasn't willing to accept that just yet. I was still adjusting to my new reality: that a specter from my audition was suddenly here in San Francisco, taking over the track I had spent two months learning.

In other words, I'd been replaced. And the gears kept moving.

"Mm, Pirate's Booty," said Alyssa, reaching over my lap to the communal bowl.

As I watched her chew and talk to Etai with her mouth full, I knew that, in the end, I liked her. She was friendly, enthusiastic (giddy, even) and had a killer voice—probably one of the best I'd ever heard. What did I care that she'd replaced me? This was exciting, not something to lament. And while I still felt like a newbie myself, I'd do my best to help her along.

"I'm starting the timer, y'all," said Annie, as she waved a little game piece in the air, which looked like a mini answering machine. "Catchphrase time!"

As the shouting match began, on the TV Chris Hansen was reading from a piece of paper while a man in a cowboy hat cried into his hands. "PleasureLover1995? Is that your screen name?"

Just then I heard the distinctly French Canadian call of Nic, shouting my name ("Fel-i-sha!"), as he handed me the little screen, which said *Greece*—a word I had to get my teammates to guess.

"The Olympics?"

"Athlete!" shouted Marshall.

"Countries, world," I said.

"Nationalism!" yelled Cary.

I thought of a new tactic.

"*Summer lovin' had me a blast...*"

"Grease!" everyone shouted together.

"Yay, homonyms," I said, refreshing the screen as I handed it off to Libby, while people kept yelling and foaming at the mouth. I wondered if they, like me, had grown up with board games and sing-alongs as foundations for their every social encounter. Based on their intense (some might say "violent") level of commitment, I would guess the answer to be yes.

"Team One wins!" yelled Annie, as Etai massaged Cary's shoulders in celebration. I wasn't sure which team I had been on, so I cheered anyway. Next it was time for Scattergories, where everyone creates lists of things that start with the same letter.

While Annie distributed pens and paper, I caught wind of Etai and Alyssa, murmuring together in the corner.

"Did you talk to her?" whispered Alyssa.

"Yeah—she said she might stop by," answered Etai.

"Who?" I asked.

"Eden," they said in unison.

"Eden?"

"Did you hear? She lives in this building," said Libby, who had also been listening.

"Really?" I said.

Yes, Libby confirmed, Eden lived right down the hall.

"Oh, cool," I said nonchalantly, while in my mind I was breakdancing in the style of M.C. Hammer.

How could I not? Hearing that Eden lived down the hall was like learning the White House was on my block, and I might get to trick-or-treat there. Scratch that—that the president might trick-or-treat *here!*

Because Eden Espinosa, Broadway legend, was maybe going to play board games with us.

As I continued to mentally breakdance, Scattergories began, which meant more yelling and mouth-foaming. By the end of the first round, Marshall had taken a two-point lead—because, for "Things You Plug In," he'd written *mammogram machine.*

"Nice!" said Nic.

He gave Marshall a high five, then said:

"Boobs."

A new round began. I could tell the competition was serious, but then again, so was the bonding. Marshall and French Nic discovered that they loved not only boobs but also working out, and so scheduled some man-time together at the gym. Annie and I interrogated Alyssa about tea steeping, since she was an apparent connoisseur, while Libby and Cary browsed through an *Us Weekly* magazine, featuring cover-model Nicole Ritchie, circa the Skeletor Years. Meanwhile, Etai floated around grabbing everyone's elbow skin, which he called a "weenus," pinching us to attention at the start of each round.

"The letter is W."

We started scribbling with our mini pencils, but I was too distracted to concentrate.

Eden Espinosa! At board game night!

I glanced back up at the TV, where Chris Hansen was holding a rolled-up packet of papers over his head, as if to strike.

Nic spoke after two minutes. "Okay, Boys Names."

"William Wallace," said Marshall, at which point Nic gave him another high five.

"Does that have anything to do with boobs?" I asked.

"It's two points," Marshall called to me, "and totally badass."

"Woodrow Wilson!" shouted Cary, in retaliation.

"Wan?" said Libby, reading from her scrap of paper.

"You spell 'Juan' with a J!" shouted Cary.

"You *could* spell it with a W!" I yelled back, defending my standby wife.

Through the shouting hardly anybody heard the knock at the door.

"Eden!" Libby squealed.

As if by magic, the woman called Eden Espinosa was in our mortal midst. Forget the president—she was an Olympian goddess, greeting and walking among the Athenian citizens. That's right: Eden Espinosa. At board game night. Theater dorks everywhere were peeing their high-waisted tights.

"Hey, guys," she said simply.

"Hello!" we all yelled.

For an Olympian she dressed simply, with a blazer, gingham button-down, cuffed jeans, and sparkly flats. Holding her hand was a man, bearded and in a tweed jacket (Zeus?), whose eyes were darting around the room—which, with paper, popcorn, and shoes strewn everywhere, looked like a fourth-grade classroom.

Eden spoke again.

"Hope we aren't interrupting anything!"

At which point we all burst into laughter, even though nothing about what she had said was a joke.

Libby offered to take her coat, explaining that we were in the middle of a heated Scattergories game, and would they like something to eat, or maybe drink, and how about a grape? But Eden declined, explaining that she and her fiancé Joseph—the Zeus on her arm—were just stopping by after an evening out.

To prolong her visit, I sprang up to introduce her to Marshall. "Eden, you need to meet my boyfriend!"

I grabbed Marshall by the collar and shoved him in the general direction of the door, while my mouth kept talking.

"How are you, by the way? Good? Nice night, isn't it? Did you guys go out? Where did you go?"

I was badgering the witness; luckily, Marshall was there to object.

"Hi! I'm Marshall, ha ha, it's so nice to meet you, ha ha," he said, extending his massive paw, laughing the entire time.

"This is my fiancé, Joseph."

Marshall shared a forearm-flexing handshake with Joseph, all the while saying to Eden, "You know, I almost hit you with my chair in Starbucks! And then after I did—I mean, I *didn't* actually hit you, but, I mean, after I *almost* did, ha ha—Felicia was like 'that's Eden Espinosa' and I couldn't believe it, ha ha!"

I started laughing like a hyena.

"Oh, Marsh, no need to tell her about that, ha ha!"

The Game Night pride joined in behind me, overcome by a fit of high-pitched laughter. (Apparently all of us coped with being star-struck the exact same way.)

Next came Annie, paying due respects to the Olympians, while Marshall and I remained at attention like puppies on our hind legs.

But in a blink, Eden and Joseph were floating around the room, saying their goodbyes before heading back toward the door.

As Eden turned to go, I called out to her.

"So, I'll see you next week?"

"Right," said Eden, cocking her head. "For...?"

"Oh, ha ha," I said, laughing like a hyena imitating a crazier hyena, "I'll be trailing you backstage. I think it's Friday night? Anyway, I think that's when it is. Ha ha!"

"Oh, right! Awesome. See you later, guys."

She and Joseph disappeared around the corner.

The door shut, and we sat in silence, while Chris Hansen gazed directly into the camera, pointed a finger at us, and said, "You *will* be caught."

Several minutes passed, and Etai was the first to speak.

"She's hot."

Nic high-fived him.

"You're filthy," was all I could say.

But it was true. She *was* hot.

She was *more* than hot.

She was Eden Espinosa!

13. HAPPY TRAILING

Through the white mist of two humidifiers, I watched as Eden adjusted her black braided wig, while the makeup artist dabbed her face, neck, and hands with gobs of translucent powder, which puffed out in all directions before dissolving into thin air.

"To set the green," he explained.

Tonight was the night I would be trailing Eden backstage, as I'd done with Laura for my ensemble track. Instead of performing, I'd been "swung out" for the evening, which meant one of the swings would be covering my track. My goal that night was to observe Eden's every move—silent and undetected, without getting in her way. (More or less like I'd done in Starbucks.)

Eden sat plainly, her hands folded on her lap, while she chatted with the wig supervisor about the weather, their day off, the price of gas—casual, polite fare. Since half-hour she'd been sitting calmly while others buzzed around her, worker bees tending to the queen.

Meanwhile, I was feet away, examining every line, crevice, ridge, and valley on her face, as the makeup designer carried out the transformative ritual.

Averting my eyes, I noticed a Michael Jackson poster hanging above a mini fridge and a small blue couch, the only piece of furniture in the room besides Eden's swivel chair and the stool someone had brought in for me. Despite the office ceiling tiles and stark white walls, it felt like Eden had done her best to make the space her own, hanging a curtain in front of the bathroom door and taping pictures of her family and fiancé on the mirror.

As I turned back to watch Eden, I was struck by her level of calm. I think I half-expected something theatrical to happen. I wasn't sure what. Chanting? Yoga poses? A ceremony involving incense and a slaughtered goat?

At the very least I expected some kind of warm-up. When had she found time to prepare?

I decided to ask, my voice wobbly through bashfulness.

"Uh, Eden—how early do you usually get here?"

Eden spoke in a deep, placid voice.

"I like to give myself fifteen to thirty minutes—so, like, 7:15 at the latest."

"Oh, cool," I said, surprised that this was all the time she needed.

"But, see, when I first did the role," she continued, "I would arrive, like, two hours early. To prepare. Now, not so much." At this, she craned her neck toward me, and we locked eyes.

"It gets to be...a lot."

"I can imagine," I said, with a nervous smile—even though, for all my rehearsing, I could *not* imagine. Nothing could prepare me for the actual *feeling* of going onstage, in front of thousands, in my newly greened skin.

Just then, a petite woman with brown wavy hair and apple cheeks walked in. Her name was Kathleen and she was Elphaba's dresser.

"Are you excited for your put-in?" she said in my direction as she pieced through the garment rack behind me, taking quick inventory of that evening's costumes.

"In a sense," I said.

"We'll be getting to know each other real soon," she said as she headed to the door, scooping up the black witch's hat that had been placed over an orange traffic cone.

Through the dressing room monitor I heard the "places" call, and watched as the wig guy carefully positioned Eden's two microphones under her wig—an extra one for backup—inching them out onto her forehead. Soon Kathleen was back, helping Eden with her wool blazer, handing off her prop glasses.

Then, one by one, the crew left the room.

"Have a great show," they each said.

"Want me to duck out?" I asked, unsure if I would be imposing on Eden's final moments.

"Nah, you can stay. Just don't mind me."

At this, she let loose a deafening vocal siren that soared from the top of her range all the way down to the bottom. This, too, she did with absolute calm—while looking in the mirror and placing her wireframe glasses on the bright green bridge of her nose.

Together we heard the preshow announcement and the orchestra's overture, signaling the show's beginning.

The *Wicked* cogs had been set in motion.

"Do you, uh, ever get nervous?" I said.

Eden smiled. "Me? No." She squirted what looked like vocal spray into her mouth. "It's something else. Hard to explain."

Through the speakers Glinda's soprano floated above the orchestra, while Eden busted out even more strange inhuman vowels. As time marched on, I suddenly felt myself sweating, as if I were somehow the one going on.

If it's this bad now...

The opening number was drawing to a close, but still Eden remained firmly planted; fishing in her blazer pockets, dusting off the wool fabric. As the ensemble concluded the number—belting the word "wicked" one, two, three times, like a harmonious fog horn—Eden, without warning, opened her mouth and sang along to the final blast, belting out the highest note I had ever heard coming from anyone.

"*WIIIIICKEEEEEEEED!*"

Then, after a brief pause:

"Okay," she said. "Let's do this."

I followed her through the dressing room door.

Tonight, I would cast a blind eye on my 3F track and faithfully and obsessively observe everything Eden did, like a German shepherd, or Glenn Close in *Fatal Attraction*.

Watching someone do something you didn't understand was like listening to a group of people speak rapid-fire in a foreign language. From conjugated verbs to idiomatic phrases, I needed to crack the code behind Eden's performances—taking note of where she set her vocal spray, in what order she pulled on her knee pads, the exact manner she would drape her prop knapsack over her shoulder. Everything mundane was spellbinding.

In between scenes, Eden offered me little tips here and there, narrating what she was doing and why. Meanwhile, Kathleen performed all sorts of magical quick changes, handing off her water bottle or a bunch of props, while the wig guy would fuss with the Elphaba wig (pinning it into its various hairstyles and configurations) and the makeup guy appeared out of nowhere to retouch her makeup, re-sponge her hands, or dab a tiny paintbrush onto her nose.

Watching all this confirmed that in the world of mega professional theater, everything was laid out for you—pre-positioned just-so to make life easy. In high school, college, or other non-professional productions, nine times out of ten you were in charge of your own makeup, hair, quick changes, and props—the silent tasks that, together, doubled the work of performing a role. To me, it was the difference between cooking a meal on your own, or starring in a Food Network show. When you cooked for yourself, it was a labor of love—but then it took longer, and at what cost? A burnt morsel here, some heavy seasoning there. But on TV, your ingredients were prepared for you by invisible helpers—finely chopped and sorted into cute little ceramic bowls, while you got to cook for everybody with ease and authority.

The point is: it helps to have help.

Onstage, Elphaba was one person. Offstage, she was a team. She was makeup retouches, water bottles, swatches of wool, knee pads. Endurance. Stamina. Focus. Calculations and preparations. It was all so cohesive. One missed cue, broken zipper, or misplaced prop could snowball into who knows how big a derailment.

I realized that being a professional didn't mean being wholly self-sufficient. When I would play Elphaba (should the day come), I would be able to rely on others.

And others would rely on me.

Eden dashed onstage, and I turned to watch her from my post in the wings. All at once I saw her, so vividly, as Elphaba—the young student, overlooked by her family, still hopeful for the future—of her calling to "make good," as it said in the *Wicked* script. From song to song, her vocal acrobatics unfolded before me. Soon she was in the home stretch of Act I, a juggernaut of scene-after-scene, with only 20 seconds offstage for a quick costume change—all leading up to the Act I finale.

Crouching on an offstage staircase in the most downstage wing, I peered out at the action. From my position, I couldn't see the audience—only the performers—and if I really let go, I almost felt like I was among them.

Like I was Elphaba Thropp, brave and uncompromising.

❖   ❖   ❖

David 8:40 PM hello there – come backstage – she is not sure she is going to stay in. we will know more soon

A week and a half later—my very first day as standby—and the Big Day had arrived, nothing like I'd imagined it.

I hustled through the wings, skin smeared in green, moments away from my Elphaba debut—a mid-Act I swap, right before "Defying Gravity."

Every image whizzed by, like scenery past a runaway train—with green-tinted windows. Though surrounded by people, I felt so inconsolably alone, trying to ignore the chatter of voices in my head. I needed to release myself from the stronghold of self-doubt and become someone else entirely. To become—

Without warning, Eden appeared, and I launched myself onto the stage, a wind-up toy giving its first mechanical lurch.

Oh God, what is happening.

Soon I was staring off into the blackness, blinded by the lights, staggered by the shock of being inside what felt like someone else's skin. But, somehow, I was talking, walking, and singing, my right brain puppeteering my marionette strings so that, by some invisible force, I was able to perform.

My gaze swept over the Orpheum Theater, and in its place I began to imagine the Emerald City—its buildings, its streets, its people. I felt my right brain move me, to and fro, in and out of reality, until I was nearing the finale.

Why did it have to be mid-show, right before "Defying Gravity?"

The most treacherous Song of Death!

Just breathe.

As its climax approached, I stood dead center, gripping Glinda's hand while we sang in unison, bidding each other farewell. Our palms slid past one another as I started to back up, running through the pre-flying sequence in my head.

Broom left...satchel right...upstage cross...

Gripping my broom, I turned my back to the audience and groped for the satchel's clasp with sweaty fingers.

C'mon!

The stubborn thing wouldn't open. I kept ducking upstage and to the left, wondering if I should just head back anyway.

I was running out of time.

Finally, the satchel came undone and I bolted back. Holding my broom, as I charged forward I was suddenly stopped—dead in my tracks. Again, I tried to walk, but I was stuck.

I looked down to see it: my broom had gotten caught between two set pieces, a barrier stretching horizontally across the tiny space I was supposed to walk through. I tried to rotate the broom so it was vertical, but the flood of music and threat of missing my cue kept my body propelling forward, my hips pressing squarely onto the long broom handle.

C'mon!

I was locked at a standstill—a bicyclist who'd made a wrong turn down a one-way street—but still I kept pushing, riding against the traffic, looking for a way to veer around it. The music was racing, and if my right brain didn't tell me to do something, the entire show would grind to a halt.

I smashed my body forward.

Thwack!

The broom snapped in half, its pieces—handle and straw head—landing on the stage with two pathetic little *thuds*.

(YOUNGER READERS: EARMUFFS!)

"Fuck!" I said through a gasp, praying for the love of all that was family-friendly that my microphone had been turned off.

No time to think.

Right brain, go!

I scrambled for the head of the broom, leaving the handle on the ground, and stepped back for takeoff. Before I knew what was happening, I was soaring above the stage, clenching my butt and waving the half-broom—like a defiant cleaning lady brandishing her dustpan brush.

I was floating, clenching, wailing to the sweet high heavens, which at that moment felt close enough to touch—or, even better, clean. Half-broom in hand, sweat pouring down my face, I knew I looked ridiculous. But I didn't care.

Elphaba didn't care. She was free, she was flying, she was never looking back—or down, for that matter.

Holy crap, it's a long way down.

ACT TWO.
OVER THE RAINBOW

&

GREEN

/grin/ *adjective*

6. having a sickly appearance; pale: *green with fear.*

7. freshly slaughtered or still raw: *green meat.*

8. freshly set and not completely hardened: *green cement.*

9. untrained; inexperienced: *a green understudy.*

14. I DON'T WANNA GROW UP

Email from Esa to Felicia.

Hi Felicia,

I am a *Wicked* fan and an avid follower of your blog, which, I might add, is HILARIOUS. I was hoping you might have an idea of when you might be going on as Elphaba? I know in a post from last month you noted that you would let us know if you have prior knowledge of an upcoming performance, so I wanted to email you to let you know that I would DEFINITELY want to know when this date may be as I would love to come out to support you!!

Also, in reading through fans' blogs, I heard that you performed for the first time tonight. CONGRATULOTIONS!!! I'm sure you were fantastic!!

Thank you!
Esa

I woke the next morning facedown in a wet, green-smeared pillow—my head throbbing, my back in knots.

Fumbling with my glasses, I trudged to the bathroom, where in the mirror a droopy-eyed girl stared back at me. She had a green forest hairline, surrounded by a nest of blonde curly fries, which in the night had sprung up to frame her face in the style of Shirley Temple, if Shirley Temple had ever taken a mug shot for DUI.

Cowering away, I sleepwalked to the coffee maker, where I got a slow drip going. As I did, images from the prior night began to drift back, like the vague memory of nightmare.

Holy crap, it's a long way down.

Had it been real?

The green in my hair, orbiting my ears, and caked in my nails was evidence that, yes, the worst-case scenario had come true: on my very first day as standby, I'd been called on, mid-show, and— *did I break the broom right before "Defying Gravity?"*

As I reached for the coffee to pour myself a mug, I tried to come up with a worthy analogy.

Jumping on as Elphaba, mid-show, on my very first day, had been like...

Climbing Everest.

When I'd only just learned to walk.

Because how could it possibly get worse?

I sipped my coffee as if in slow motion—my grip weak, my arm shaky.

Seriously. You couldn't make this stuff up.

A moment later and my phone began buzzing.

"David?"

"Great job last night!"

"Oh, thanks," I said hoarsely. How nice, I thought, that the stage manager was calling to check up on me.

"Also, you're on for both shows!"

I froze.

"What?"

"Eden will be out for both today, so it's all you."

"Wait, *what?*"

(**GREEN.** 6. having a sickly appearance; pale; *green with fear*.)

"I'll meet you in the dressing room for notes," said David. "See you at half-hour."

I'd asked it, and now I had my answer. How could it possibly get worse?

Two shows. One day.

What. The. Eff.

I hung up the phone and sat on the couch.

Then I started to laugh.

Then I started to cry.

Day One's Everest Climb, you see, had been a mere primer for Day Two's endurance test. The itinerary? A matinee followed by an evening show. (Double the Elphaba, double the fun!)

Forget Everest; this was worse. This was Mount Elphaba.

"How does anyone *do* this," I wailed to Kathleen as we scurried backstage like blind mice, trying to pace through costume changes we'd rehearsed only a few times. "It doesn't seem possible!"

As I sweated my way through the matinee, I gulped compulsively from my Nalgene, trying to replenish the dwindling water supply escaping from my pits, while meanwhile I had to incorporate David and Bryan's many notes from Day One—which they'd told to me while I was getting green, minutes before "places."

As the curtain fell on my second Elphaba show, not only was I exhausted, but my vocal cords felt like they'd been set on fire. What's more, there was no real relief—only the foreboding knowledge that I'd have to do my Mount Elphaba climb all over again—in a mere three hours.

To coat my throat and make the singing more manageable, I stuck pastilles between my teeth and cheeks and left them there for the evening show. As I huffed around onstage, wheezing and panting, my mouth began to feel numb, tingling with minty-fresh paralysis, while meanwhile I tried not to choke each time I inhaled.

With fried cords and a slack jaw, during my third pass at Elphaba, I couldn't help but wonder, Would the Songs of Death live up to their names?

In the throes of self-pity, to me it wasn't a matter of *if*; it was only a matter of *when*.

Cause of Death: Musical Theater.

Yes, at any moment I would transubstantiate into *Wicked*'s first martyr. Like a green Joan of Arc, with a better singing voice. (Although, who knows? Maybe Joan of Arc could *belt her face*.) At my death, all the villagers would crowd around my lifeless body. "Good news," they would say, "she's dead."

That night, as my wet-haired head hit the pillow, I knew I had to look on the bright side.

After a two-show Wednesday, my second day on the job, how could it *possibly* get worse?

I woke Day Three with a needling pain in my throat. As I moved to swallow, I felt a sea of bacteria envelop my vocal cords, lapping around in a whirlpool of mucus that churned as far as my head, sinus, and chest.

Uh oh.

Why now? Since arriving in San Francisco, I hadn't taken a single sick day. And today couldn't be worse timing.

Wicked had found itself in an uncommonly vulnerable position—with only one person (me) covering Elphaba, as opposed to two. With all the recent casting changes, Alyssa was our new understudy but was still in the process of learning the role—and was, at best, weeks away from being ready.

So there was only one backup plan.

And that backup plan had gotten sick.

I concluded that the bacteria must have done their due diligence. Obviously they'd staged a sneak attack, at precisely the worst moment—knowing that when I'm stressed, one little throat tickle could turn into a holocaust on my cords and, in turn, my confidence.

The smart bastards!

First they'd poisoned my throat; soon they'd poison my mind.

They never should have hired you.

Cannons raging.

Face it, Felicia: You won't be able to do this.

Incoming!

You. Are. Going. To—

Enough!

I began rocking on my couch in the fetal position, waiting for the heavens to deliver some kind of sign.

Felicia: 11:57AM Any word from Eden on how she's feeling, or is it too early?

As I waited to hear back from David, I felt sicker and sicker—while the stakes kept mounting higher and higher.

Heck, I needed a miracle!

Since I'd survived the Songs of Death (so far), I hadn't earned musical theater martyr status (yet)—so to conjure said miracle I'd have to enlist outside help.

By the power of Shoshana? Of Eden herself?

No, other Elphabas hit too close to home. I needed to go back further...to those golden years of musical theater obsession...

Are you there, Douglas Sills? It's me, Felicia.

When I was 12 I gave you a calendar outside the Minskoff Theatre in which every month was a picture of your face. You gave me a hug, told me you loved it, and that you'd send it to your mom (which I hope you did, since what mother wouldn't love clocking the forward march of time with the aid of her son's giant face?).

At final count, my dad and I saw you as Percy in The Scarlet Pimpernel *ten times (eight times on Broadway, two times on tour) and I can wager with confidence that you never made a single mistake, not even when you belted such absurdly high notes in your tight English revolutionary pants that I thought you might just combust into a flaming musical theater sun—which had absolutely nothing to do with the fact that the character of Percy was an incredibly flaming, albeit heterosexual individual. No, your fireball of talent burned bright, independent of all ambiguous sexuality and foppishness.*

Indeed, you were there for me, Douglas, in the toughest of times— in middle school when I had lice (twice) and had to chop off my hair; when I fell in love with my gay best friend Patrick, who ran off with my other gay best friend Jon, all in the same year that I didn't get cast in summer camp; on the dark day you left The Scarlet Pimpernel *and I saw your replacement Ron Bohmer by accident, who was small and inadequate. (All right, Ron Bohmer was fine. But I couldn't get behind him morally—due to my allegiance to you and also because of the cover photo of his solo album, in which a long rattail flows down his back. I mean, what purported leading man would willingly have hair like that? Certainly not you.)*

Anyway, Douglas, if you're listening: please help. Teach me to pull through! Teach me to shoulder the pressures of being an actor! Teach me to maintain the tautest of posteriors! (Were your glutes so supple from onstage butt-clench singing, or was it genetic? Because you really did have a fantastic man-butt.)

Lastly, please, oh please, make Eden get better. It is my only hope tonight, since I have no understudy, and each time I try to sing I sound like a bullfrog suffering at the hand of a bigger bullfrog, who is tormenting the smaller bullfrog because she is a terrible singer, even for a bullfrog. If Eden calls out, oceans will rise, buildings will crumble, and/or Wicked *will have to be canceled. Please don't let that happen,*

Douglas! I'm just a lowly, newly turned professional actress, who wants at all costs to avoid being shamed and/or the public enemy of Wicked *fans the world over.*

Please?

Alternatively, if you can do none of these things, could you send me a signed headshot? I'm at 466 Clementina Street, Apt 2, San Francisco, CA, 94103.

Sincerely, Felicia

P.S. For years I have wished you were (1) not two decades older than me, (2) my husband. Just needed to get that off my chest. Because if I don't take this opportunity to blatantly proposition you, what would even be the point of this prayer?

And, praise Douglas! Four more hours of rocking in the fetal position, and the miracle came—in the form of a text.

David: 4:54 PM Just got word that she is in tonight.

Hallelujah!

(Celebrity obsession *can* have a practical application!)

I felt so happy I could cry. So, obviously I did: big, goopy tears. The kind that comes from your eyes *and* your nose.

That evening in the standby dressing room I went on complete vocal rest, as indicated by the construction paper sign I'd fashioned with magic marker. CAN'T TALK, it said, with a frowny face. I held it tightly near my chest as I lay on the couch next to my humidifier, which I'd positioned to blast directly into my goop-filled nostrils. Libby sat on the other side of the room doing a puzzle of Rockefeller Center at Christmastime. We'd silently agreed it was best she kept her distance from me—a vessel of illness and despair.

Like a vulture sniffing out a carcass, Etai soon appeared and proceeded to grab my weenus, trying to get me to laugh. I hated (but secretly loved) this weenus bit of his, so it was a testament to my Joan of Arc will that I resisted.

Once Etai left, through the dressing room monitor I could hear Eden onstage, powering through the songs. She sounded fine. But—

My teeth chattered. Might she call out mid-show—again? This was the demon that lurked in the corner opposite Libby, doing its own puzzle, which, when assembled, depicted: Felicia's Failure.

But, lo!

Eden pulled through, and I survived the night in one piece.

Thank you, thank you, thank you, Douglas Sills!

(P.S. Call me.)

Day Four was anybody's guess. Would Eden call out?

It was all I kept wondering (and, incidentally, all I would keep wondering every single day and night I spent in San Francisco, as it haunted my standby dreams).

I'd used up my musical theater miracle, and had no other choice but to prepare for the worst—gargling buckets of salt water, hoping I could maybe dislodge the phlegm that was holding my vocal cords hostage.

In the afternoon, I got official word.

David: 2:10PM you are green tonight – please confirm

Crap.

I'd thought I'd reached my peak, but I'd have to keep climbing Mount Elphaba. The trails kept materializing into the sky, and for my fourth show—my third day on the job—I would have to perform slightly sick.

Felicia: 2:11PM Confirmed!

David: 2:11PM Come in a little early for notes and stuff!

More improvements. More tweaks. More trails.

David: 2:37PM looks like libby is on so we need to do fight call as well

My standby wife!

We'd never performed together, so this meant a whole new set of firsts or, through a pessimist's eyes, things to worry about. At least we'd meet for a "fight call" before the show to rehearse a few choreographed moments.

David: 4:33PM So confirming 6p for vocals and 7p for slap that witch.

"Vocals" meant Bryan and I would do some pre-show cleanup, while "slap that witch" was stage manager lingo for a scene with Libby in Act II, full of wrestle-tussling and—you guessed it— witches slapping each other.

Felicia: 4:34PM Both are confirmed

I took a deep breath.

I chugged five glasses of water.

I ate a banana.

I rehearsed with Bryan.

I slapped that witch.

Then?

I climbed Mount Elphaba.

(Again!)

And—Songs of Death be damned! I made it out alive.

❖   ❖   ❖

Over 40 performances later, I learned that playing Elphaba evoked many different feelings.

But that first week? I could boil it down to two:

1) *HolycrapIamplayingmydreamrole!*

2) *This sucks so hard.*

One minute, I was soaring from the freeing rush of being onstage; the next, I was in a whimpering heap.

I'd never before sympathized with crack addicts, but after my debut week felt kindred to the poor fraught souls who lived outside my door. (It's true: Marshall and I often found crack pipes on our stoop.) You might also think of me as a big rubber band: each show, I got stretched to my limit; afterwards, I snapped back on myself. When withdrawal set in, I'd never felt so low—my arms, legs, neck, and shoulders ached from the incredible exertion of playing Elphaba.

After the final recoil, the sun set on Sunday, and Marshall and I cooked a pork chop feast, toasting with wine (him) and lemon water (me) the long-awaited end to my week. After Friday night's semi-sick performance, I'd had one more peak to scale: a fifth Elphaba show for the Saturday matinee.

"At 23," Marshall began, "you've done it. You've played Elphaba five times!"

I did a golf clap, almost tipping over my glass.

"I think you can retire now, from everything," he said, "and move to a remote island."

"You are right," I said. "But before that I have to tick off a few other items on my list, including inventing a way to read in bed, without hands." (I'd been scheming to build this contraption since I was eight: it would involve metal beams, Plexiglass, and a computer chip in your brain so you could lie on your back, gaze up at the pages suspended above you, and command that they turn only by thinking it.)

"Oh, and I also want to write a book."

"Fair enough."

I wolfed down a morsel of pork doused in a balsamic-shallot reduction—a recipe Marshall had concocted from scratch.

"So now what?" he asked, taking a large bite.

Now what?

If I thought about it, this "you've done it" idea was slightly unsettling. Because now, you see, I had to keep going—for nearly six months—as Elphaba standby in *Wicked*.

Would things get easier? Or would Mount Elphaba tower higher, colder, and with thinner air?

It was hard to know.

But what were the odds that *Wicked* could get any more difficult?

Just keep climbing.

"Now—" I said with a sigh, "now I'm going to bed."

On a soggy, green-smeared pillow.

❖   ❖   ❖

A few days later, and I was on YouTube singing "Defying Gravity" for the all the free world (or at least my mother) to see.

"Oh my God, it's incredible," she said to me over the phone. "I posted it on Facebook."

Yes, these were the facts. I hadn't yet scrubbed off all the green, but already I was online, shrunken to mini proportions, performing for home viewers at the mere click of a mouse. Documented and cataloged, for posterity. And belting contests.

In short, I had been YouTube-ized—by a really efficient bootlegger.

(**GREEN**. 7. freshly slaughtered or still raw: *green meat.*)

"Great video," chimed my dad who was, as usual, listening in on the other line.

"Oh, hi, dad."

To change the subject, I told my parents that I was on my way to the mall to find a new computer bag. As I'd spent more time blogging, I'd been lugging my laptop to the theater in a Trader Joe's tote, which simply would not do for an established woman of letters.

"You're taking a cab, I hope?" asked my mother, who had heard tales from past sidewalk safaris.

"Nah, it's close enough to walk," I said, scanning my surroundings.

Marshall and I had recently moved from the dilapidated comforts of the Hunky House to a new apartment ten minutes from the mall and the Orpheum Theater. This meant we'd traded neighbors Tom, Etai, David, and Tim for the colorful inhabitants of Market Street.

"Always stay safe," said my dad.

"It's fine," I said. "Right now, for example, there's a woman sitting in a shopping cart in the middle of the street. Directing traffic."

"Why are there so many homeless people over there?" asked my mom.

"I'm not sure," I said. "I read somewhere that the city is underfunded, and can't support many civil services or outreach programs."

"Double-lock your doors!" shouted my father.

My parents were overreacting; here, in our new hood, Marshall and I were part of a close-knit community. Many folks even lived and slept right outside our door. These *literal* next-door neighbors were very friendly, since they often left us little gifts of crack pipes and used toilet paper.

Why the free and willing move near Market Street? For one thing, Marshall and I were lured by our new apartment's finishes, washer-dryer, and kitchen sink that didn't double as the bathtub. Second (and more importantly) it turned out that *Wicked* would allow its standbys to leave the theater during the show—as long as they stayed within five blocks. With my recent promotion, I could arrive at work, sign in, and retrace the five blocks to my apartment—watching TV, cleaning, or blogging—while keeping my cell phone close in case the theater needed me.

In summary, our new place near Market Street meant I could go home during work, wear clean clothes, and greet strange men as they peed outside my garage.

"Anyway, I think I'm going to try the Fossil store, since they had some good bags," I said.

"Try TJ Maxx," said my dad.

"Is somebody screaming in the background?" asked my mother.

Three drivers were honking their horns and sticking their heads out the window, yelling at the shopping cart lady, who was now eating a bag of chips.

"No."

"Well, make sure you go to YouTube when you get home."

"Okay, Mom."

"I'm going to email you the link," said my dad, "so you can see it for yourself."

"Which performance is it, anyway?" I asked, feeling a tug of regret.

"It said it was your third full performance," answered my mother.

"Oh, great, the night I was sick," I said.

"Honey, you *do not* sound sick!"

"Mom, it's okay, you don't have to—"

"You are the *best Elphaba!*"

"I just love those high notes at the end," said my dad, as he explained that the clip was of me singing the "Defying Gravity" finale—those final notes of doom.

"Oh, it's not the whole song?" I said, feigning surprise.

Really, I knew better. From my own YouTube searches (guilty as charged) I'd seen that most *Wicked* bootlegs only bothered to capture the ending. Over and over I'd watched my favorite actresses, as recently as a few months before, *belting their faces* for hours on end.

But that was then! And this was now. Now, the tables had turned.

"Are you going to read the comments?" asked my mother.

"The what?"

"The YouTube comments!"

"I commented," said my dad.

"Me, too!" said my mom.

"No, probably not," I said.

"Why not?"

Because it could get ugly, I wanted to say. Because people are made boldly cruel by their anonymity. Because I could predict, even before logging on, the three things they would say:

1) That was good.

2) That was bad.

3) So-and-So was better.

Instead I settled on: "Because I can't read."

"Just make sure you take a look," said my dad. "Or I could read them for you right now."

Ah, make it stop!

"Enough!" I screeched.

As I watched the shopping cart lady take out a soda can and start to chug I felt a twinge of remorse. I knew my parents were just excited and proud. Who was I to judge them? This was how live theater worked nowadays. Thanks to the Internet, they could get a 90-second glimpse of my performance. Over and over and over.

"Sorry," I said, lightly. "It's nice of you to tell me I did a good job."

"Any definite dates when you'll go on?" asked my dad.

"No. Not yet, anyway."

"Well, let us know if you hear anything," said my mother.

"I will," I said. "Anyway, I think I gotta go."

I'd finally bypassed the shopping cart jam and arrived at the mall.

"You be careful," said my mother. "Take your vitamins— including fish oil! It decreases inflammation."

"Let me know if you need me to prescribe you antibiotics," said my father.

(Doctor parents.)

"Okay! Love you!"

I'd taken the mall escalator up a few flights to the Fossil store, where I started browsing leather totes. In the calm of the air-conditioned space I was glad to leave all discussions of Elphaba, *Wicked*, and YouTube behind.

Here, it was just me and my wallet. And some hard-earned shopping therapy.

As I picked up a satchel made from distressed leather, feeling its weight in my hands, a salesperson approached.

"Excuse me," he said.

I looked up and saw a young man with frosted tips and a blue-checkered tie.

"Oh, I'm just looking, thanks."

Next I moved to a bag that looked like a convertible backpack, only with longer straps. I peeled aside the tag to check the price.

"No, I was just wondering," the salesperson said as I fingered the snaps, "are you in *Wicked*?"

I stopped.

"Oh," I said, turning to face him. "Yes, I am."

His gaze shot up to my green hairline, then back to my eyes.

"I think I saw you this week!"

"Oh, ha ha, no way," I said, looking down at the floor.

"It's one of my favorite shows," he said.

"Me, too," I said.

I crossed to the other end of the store, where I steered the conversation toward a couple of bags. Together we weighed the pros and cons of more or less pockets, long or short straps, leather or nylon. I draped one over my shoulder and backed up to look in the full-length mirror.

"Let me tell you—"

"Do you think it looks good?" I asked, turning sideways for a profile view.

"I just want to say: you can really belt your face."

Seriously?

"Hey, thanks," I said, with a hollow laugh. "That's really nice of you."

I decided on leather with pockets, swiped my credit card, and braved the streets home.

Later that evening, I gave in.

Marshall was asleep, so I locked myself in my bathroom, took my computer out of its leather pouch (with pockets), and groped my electronic way to YouTube, with the volume set as low as possible. There I found the infamous video in question.

Defying Gravity – Felicia Ricci | 427 views

I was scared.

Any mistakes I'd made were now permanent. Any flubs, careless errors, unsupported notes that fell under pitch—these were wounds that would be salted anytime someone clicked "play."

I wanted to watch. But something was holding me back.

I thought back to my conversation with Etai over breakfast-for-dinner—about how musical theater shouldn't be a pissing contest to see who could be the *best*. It wasn't a competitive sport. It wasn't something to be replayed, labeled, and judged. But on YouTube, comparisons were contagious. Often they mutated beyond the comments realm into their own strain of online cancer: the video "contests," or back-to-back clips of a bunch of

Elphabas singing the same part of one song—say, a riff in "Defying Gravity" or the end of "The Wizard and I." The video's description would stipulate its charge: that it was a faceoff to determine who was the "best" when it came to riffing, hitting high notes, etc.

Pressing play, you heard only a sliver of each actress's performance, nearly indistinguishable from all the others.

Funny how a role as complex as Elphaba could be reduced to a mere five seconds.

This bugged me. Plain and simple. But was there something else?

I had played Elphaba. Thousands of people had seen me, Fossil bag dude had recognized me, 427 people had watched me on YouTube (well, 327, since 100 views were on account of my parents).

I guess I felt like—

Like I'd grown up or something.

Wicked was a fantasy I'd been reaching for since I first unclenched my little sophomore buttocks. In those early moments, I'd set my sights on the impossible dream of playing Elphaba.

Not in a million years, I'd thought.

As YouTube confirmed, this dream was not only possible, but had already come true. A million years was *now*.

So what did that mean for me?

As I saw it, there were two outcomes. One? I'd watch the video and see that I sucked. This would, in all cases, be awful. It would mean I'd achieved my goal in a truly unremarkable, or even subpar, way. And who wants that?

Two? I'd watch the video and see that, hey—I was pretty good!

This second outcome seemed better. But if I thought about it, it was actually worse.

Why? Because being good meant I—the eternal overachiever—would have to keep going: growing, evolving, working harder each day...and maintaining that high level of performance for the six months that stretched ahead.

Just keep climbing.

Was the thrill of my "greenness" gone? If yes, so was its cushy disclaimer.

(**GREEN**. 5. not fully developed or perfected in growth or condition; unripe; not properly aged: *a green actress*.)

Mount Elphaba had loomed, and I'd climbed to its highest peak.

But had I also peaked?

I clicked "play."

15. THE ELPHABA AND THE FURY

After my first unpredictable week, things gradually calmed. As time told, Eden would call out about once or twice a week (usually around the weekends, when the performance schedule was more condensed).

Despite this relative predictability, I knew never to take things for granted. Not after my debut week.

My vow?

LL101: **Always be ready, for anything**.

To stay in tip-top shape, vocal health was my religion. I held a daily Mass of shower warm-ups, with a communion of cold cure-alls, lozenges, and Manuka honey. Every night before bed and every morning when I woke up, I'd pray to the god of the Neti Pot, irrigating my browbeaten sinuses with salty water. (Picture a mini teakettle whose spout you place in one nostril while tipping it over until water comes out the other nostril. The sensation feels like drowning, but way more fun!)

This religion stayed with me wherever I went. Instead of a nun's habit, I wrapped elaborate tapestry-sized scarves around my head and neck to guard against the San Francisco wind. These scarves were practical, but also symbolic of my state of mind—one wholly dedicated to singing.

If ever I slipped (a glass of wine with dinner; dairy before performing) as penance I would drown myself in Umcka cold prevention syrup, Oscillococcinum tablets, Echinacea tea, multivitamins, and extra C supplements—hoping the evil duo of Phlegm and Congestion hadn't noticed my lapse.

But there was worthy cause for it all. I needed to be sure, beyond a doubt, that I would never get sick—ever again.

Not if I had anything to do with it!

(Cue dramatic sting!)

In the meantime, I kept working my alternately clenched and unclenched butt off, improving my Elphaba performance as best I could. Since there was only so much I could accomplish during my maintenance rehearsals—which I did out of costume, without sets or actual props—my standby performances were very much *like* rehearsals. Onstage, in front of thousands, I tried to fix my blocking, rephrase my songs, reinterpret my lines—all while in the heat of battle.

Note sessions with stage manager David and conductor Bryan followed every such Elphaba "battle." Their extensive critiques addressed all aspects of my performance. Some struck at very basic concepts ("What is your motivation?" "What emotion launches you into 'I'm Not That Girl?'"), some nitpicked ("Be sure you close your umbrella in time to hand it to Madame Morrible," "Try no vibrato on '*defying*'"), some encouraged ("Amazing work," "I'm so proud of you") and some were downright confusing ("You didn't connect with anyone onstage," "I think you were telling a different story"). Very little slipped by either of them—but especially David, whose main goal was to keep ushering me within a few centimeters of the Elphaba blocking grid.

Consistency was the name of David's game; with his mallet he chiseled me to fit the Elphaba mold.

(**GREEN.** 8. freshly set and not completely hardened: *green cement.*)

"I noticed," David said to me one day during a particularly long note session in the stage management office, "that you took your glasses off when addressing the Shiz students."

"Yes," I said.

Wanna make something of it?

He looked at me through a blank stare, barely moving as I shifted back and forth in my seat. "What was that?" he asked.

I decided to argue my case, explaining that my intention had been to shock and incite the Shiz students by showing them my green skin. I'd taken off my glasses to better display my face, direct and unobstructed, which I thought had made the action stronger.

David nodded, silently.

Sometimes he afforded me glimmers of freedom, but usually he put his foot down. Today, he took a breath and said, "Let's not do that."

"Okay," I said, as I wrote his comment on my sheet of notes. To nail the coffin shut, David added:

"It tells a different story."

Many note sessions later and I learned I needed to pick my battles. Like every long-running Broadway show, replacement actors across every *Wicked* company had to be derivative of the actors who came before them. Standbys, in particular, were coached to stay within the shadow of everything their principal actor did (for consistency and safety when interacting with other people onstage). In short, unless you were originating the role in a company and working with *Wicked*'s director Joe Mantello, there was only so much an Elphaba could do.

It wasn't about painting a new landscape; it was about coloring within the lines.

Still, I made the best of it. Each time I was lucky enough to go on, I tried to approach the role as my own—from a brand new perspective—giving it my own touch of *greenness*.

Over time, as I smoothed the edges of my Elphaba statue, the role became more manageable. I kept changing and adapting to apply David's extensive notes—much like how a weightlifter's hand sprouts a callus to guard against the chafing, or a bonsai tree curls to fit inside its tiny vase.

And as my performance changed, so did my skin.

It thickened, for one thing.

(*YouTube can kiss my ass!*)

It also changed color.

(No, seriously.)

Green pigment, you see, when applied to pasty part-Irish skin, is like grape juice on a carpet. No matter how much I scrubbed, the green would never *quite* come out. From my put-in to a month after I would play Elphaba for the last time, my face gave off a sickening, almost fluorescent glow, while impossible-to-reach patches clung around my ears and hairline, weathering even my best Q-Tip assaults.

In short, I was a giant coffee-stained tooth, if coffee were green and teeth were shaped like people.

It was a vicious cycle, too, because every time I got close to looking normal I'd get called back into the show—and the greenifying would commence.

"I look like one of those *Toy Story* alien things."

"I agree."

"You're not supposed to agree, you're supposed to tell me I look beautiful."

While non-company members usually weren't allowed backstage after half-hour, Marshall got to watch in my Elphaba dressing room before my put-in, where he proceeded to snap photos and agree that, yes, with a matte green finish and a wig cap pulled across my volleyball head, I looked positively Martian.

"Or maybe it's more like a sea creature," he said, clicking away.

It was hard to believe that this greenifying ritual would have to occur every time I went onstage but, as time told, such was the deal.

Each performance, week after week, our routine began with Elphaba dresser Kathleen—preparing my makeup, turning on my two humidifiers, and retrieving my black undergarments and green mesh jumpsuit. She'd place them next to my lukewarm (by request) water bottle and Entertainer's Secret throat spray which, together with the cardboard box I stored under the counter (with toothbrush, toothpaste, contact solution, lozenges, extra set of contacts, and deodorant) comprised my Elphaba First Aid Kit.

As the second hand ticked its way to half-hour I would scramble to get prepped in time. During these moments, while I placed my tote in the corner, hung my street clothes on a hook, and swiftly brushed my teeth, I felt kind of like an intruder. Or like I was squatting in someone else's vacation home. (Mustn't track in sand or rearrange the furniture!) Because while I was Elphaba for a day, I knew Eden would be returning soon for her extended stay.

And I would get shipped back downstairs, miles from the sun and surf.

During my cautious preparations, many people freely walked in and out of the dressing room—sometimes knocking, sometimes not. These included wardrobe people, cast members, and *Where's Waldo* Steve, who came to warn me every time he conducted.

"Need anything from me?" he would ask.

"Just, uh, conduct away!" I would reply.

And there was Libby, of course, who would usually peek in for a friendly hello before returning to the basement to work on her Christmas puzzle.

All the activity was in good spirit, but I often wished I could have some pre-show alone time to get my head on straight; as a standby, I sometimes had to go on as Elphaba without having performed it for weeks. But since interruption was the rule, not the exception, I adapted—being sure to (1) warm up, (2) go Number Two, and (3) consume obligatory banana beforehand, all in the comforts of my own apartment.

Because, at the stroke of 7:30 p.m. until moments before I would walk onstage, all privacy and solitude were surrendered. On cue, makeup designer Joe would bustle in to slather me in green, closely followed by wig supervisor Mark, who would pin my hair in loops, while Kathleen would dart around, somehow everywhere at once, appearing over my shoulder at the exact moment I needed to ask her a question ("Hey, Kathleen, could you save my prop lunch so I can eat it at intermission?").

At 7:45 p.m., stage manager David would appear along with conductor Bryan, hunching over me as they gave a few lightning-quick notes they'd forgotten to mention—while I nodded and smiled, feeling sweat forming under my armpits, above my green-tinted lip, and in my mid-back reservoir.

At 7:58 p.m., it was on with my black braided wig and Act I costume, heavy and made of wool, while Joe patted on translucent powder and sprayed my hands with fixative.

It wasn't until 8:07 p.m.—when the show actually started—that I'd be left alone.

At that moment I'd gaze in the mirror, hardly able to recognize the person staring back.

Nice to meet you, Elphaba.

The audio from the show's opening number would start to play, and I'd sing along—just as I'd seen Eden do when I first trailed her—taking those final moments to reawaken my voice, all the while trying not to worry about the challenges that lay ahead.

Like any mountain climb, I had to think of it as one foot in front of the other—*right foot, left foot*, through the dressing room door, around the bend, *right foot, left foot*, through the hanging fabric into the wings, crossing upstage to stage right, where I'd find my suitcase, pre-set for my grand Act I entrance.

I'd it pick up, cross to center, *right foot, left foot,* behind the mechanized door, where the stagehand was set to open it, precisely on cue, directly after Glinda's line...

Left brain, go!

Swing suitcase for momentum, run downstage, try not to overshoot. End center. Gaze out at Shiz University in wonder, feeling hopeful, like this new experience is full of possibility. When you hear the students start to sing, begin counting off for choreographed step sequence. Step left, right, left, turn, get cut off by crowd of people who scatter. Feel the sting of their reactions, show it in the way your body halts. Turn stage right for fainting girl. Pull yourself together. Start second step sequence, halted by upstage crowd, turn over shoulder, get startled by Boq. Upon seeing him, freeze like a statue; stamp foot to startle him. Indicate with left arm that he can pass. Cross down right and look off at fourth wall.

Upon hearing Glinda's soprano trill, turn to look. Feel the gaze of all the students. Speak first line, be sure to pace it right (not too slow). Yell, slam suitcase, charge left and confront students (keeping glasses on). Speak line about Nessarose (be sure not to rush or mumble this one). Get stopped by Father, led across stage by right arm. Reach for box; pull away hand as he snaps cover down. Cross and lean over Nessa, handing back box (do not sound self-pitying or speak line while moving box).

Reposition wheelchair more downstage during Madame Morrible's entrance. Raise hand when prompted, wait your turn. Regard Galinda, forming early opinions of her voice, her manner, her outfit. Grow impatient, raise hand again while wheeling Nessa downstage. Approach Morrible, stop when she screams. Temper sting with a joke (keep it dry). Lunge at Galinda. Consult with Nessa. Face Morrible. Feel the stakes rising. Try to stop Morrible. Feel the frustration of being dismissed.

Then explode!

Feel the relief of having Nessa by your side, and the regret of having lost control. Approach Morrible with caution. Cross right, back to Nessa, kneel by her wheelchair. Rise as Morrible approaches, cross down, take her hand. Feel stunned when she mentions the Wizard. Try to process everything as Morrible exits, turn and wave goodbye to Nessa. Hear the chords that lead into "The Wizard and I." Turn downstage to face audience in time to sing.

Start more hushed, breathe, remember to visualize everything you and Bryan discussed. Pick up suitcase and cross left, as if to exit. Get stopped by your next phrase. Put down suitcase (you can speak lyrics here), play out, pick up suitcase on low G, be sure to support with breath as you cross upstage and get stopped by crowd of students. Cross left after them, reclaiming your pride. Cross down, picturing Father, Nessa, all of Oz. Cross left, prop suitcase up, place it down to sit. Look at hands; stand. Back up, left of suitcase, then cross back down.

Grab suitcase, cross upstage (don't overshoot) while noticing a vision of your future up and to the center, hovering above the audience. Stay locked on image, while placing suitcase on moving set piece. Cross down and step on gear wheel portion of stage, describing your vision. Cross left on "celebration" (you can speak some of this), end down center. Place hands on chest, back up while singing until you hit the circular markers. Plant and sing, spreading arms from side to side. Run downstage on "melt," until front and center.

Spread arms. Hold last note, raise arms to either side, throw them down. End with arms over your head.

Or, from a different point of view:

Right brain, go!

Running, running...Didn't an Elphaba once run off the stage and land in the orchestra pit? Wow, the audience is applauding. I wonder if they think I'm Eden Espinosa. Foot cramp! Have to remember to tell Kathleen to put extra insoles in these boots. The Orpheum sure is big. I think they turned up the air conditioning tonight, it feels cooler out here, even though my wrists are sweating more than usual. I bet Joe will have to retouch the green before the school dance and—

Music cue already?!

Don't mess up these steps like you did your first week. It's left, right, left, hold...or is it the other way around? Too late. Why is it all those times I saw Teal and Eden do this opening it looked like a piece of cake? Oh, look, it's Alyssa, fainting. I remember when I used to do that part in the ensemble, right after the quick change, when my wig was barely on straight, and the bubbles from the opening number made the floor so slippery that I almost crashed into Teal. Oh, look, it's Etai. Better scare him. Ugh, I hate the way I do that. What's with my weird witch's claw and freaky face? Gotta rethink that one. Hey, look, it's the floor. Hey, look, it's Penelope. She calls me "Frishé" and that makes me feel cool.

Get ready for your first line, Fel...Should I clear my throat? This air conditioning is drying me out. Of course you can't clear your throat, you moron. My voice sounds weird right now, like an adolescent boy. Ugh, I hate the way I talk. Why didn't the audience laugh there? Gotta yell now, but I'm worried about my voice. That was lackluster. Obviously David will give me a note about not being angry enough. Should I grab Kehau's book like Teal used to do? Nah, I'll just keep my distance. Oh, look, Tim is holding my arm. His face looks stubbly today. Hey, look, it's Deedee. I saw her in Miss Saigon *once. She's the best Nessa ever and doesn't have to wear a wig, which at first I thought was lucky, but then I was like, yeah, except she has to wash her hair every time she has a performance.*

Gift box snap! Pulling my hand away feels so Vaudevillian!

Time to lean in to Deedee. I love how you can murmur onstage to the other actors and the sound designer will turn your microphone down. What should I say to her? Uh, I'll just stay in character...even though I wish I could say something hilarious, like I used to do with Kevin while Madame Morrible entered. Oh, look, there's Jody. Better keep an ear out for cues, don't want to miss your line. Time it out, roll the chair.

Libby is talking! She's on for Glinda! I nearly forgot! Look at her. I wonder if I could lift her over my head. I bet if I trained for five to ten weeks I totally could. Okay, don't make this next blocking look phony, even though it's choreographed. Get ready for the big scream. Save your voice! Too late. Ouch, my throat. Crap.

Why do I feel so dry? Did I forget to spray? I won't be able to head offstage before singing! What is happening!!! PANIC!!!

Okay, don't panic.

Kneel...talk to Deedee, try not to be all awkward and like, "I don't know what to say to you when we improvise." Here's Jody, and I guess we're downstage now. Oh God, I hate this part, when the song starts, and I know "The Wizard and I" is coming. Plus, I'm so far downstage. I can practically feel the audience's sight vectors piercing my skin. What the hell is a "sight vector?"

Bye, Nessa. Bye, everybody else onstage.

Hello, first Song of Death.

Okay, energize these notes with breath...Get out those phrases that hang in your passagio....Just ease them out. What does "making good" mean? Remember your vocal coaching! Remember that being onstage is actually less scary than getting coached by Bryan. You can do this. Ouch! Cramp! Stupid over-pronated arches!

Why do I sound like ass? I hope my head voice on "degreenify" comes out okay.

Sitting on suitcase....Sitting on suitcase. At least my foot stopped cramping. Time for the "unlimited" section. It sucks, but you've gotta do it. Back up carefully. I hope the suitcase doesn't fall with a loud boom *like it did during my put-in. See the vision of your future! Don't riff up on second "unlimited." Crossing...Get ready for the finale...Don't crack, don't crack, don't crack...Big breath! Back up to center.*

BIG HIGH NOTES! BIG HIGH NOTES! POP OUT THAT TOP NOTE! YEAH! THAT'S WHAT I'M TALKIN' BOUT!!! Now run, run, run, while singing, run, stop, hit more high notes. MORE HIGH NOTES! Don't pinch on "team!" You got it! C'mon! Just a few more! The Wizard aaaa naaaa! APPLAUD ME! APPLAUD ME, DAMMIT!!!

16. STANDING BY, PLAYING HOUSE

April 12, 2010. Felicia's Blog.

Let's get one thing straight: I love my job.

Let's get one other thing straight: sometimes it is boring. But that's okay. Lots of things that are awesome can also be boring, like the Discovery Channel, or any novel by Victor Hugo.

On days when I'm not performing, I have the privilege to wile away my hours in a shared dressing room with the impossibly delightful Libby Servais, our Glinda standby. But that's not the only thing we share! We also share laughter, tickles, secrets, rainbows, bunnies!

In all seriousness, much of being a standby consists of inventing ways to amuse oneself, while staving off the sting of existential uncertainty. Some of Libby's and my recent standby activity brainchildren include: (1) Buy complementary Snuggies and/or Slankets to lounge around in, and (2) wear in ironic glamour photo shoots; (3) Learn guitar; (4) Shampoo, comb, and style the blonde Jessica Simpson hair piece Libby inexplicably owns in order to (5) wear it in ironic glamour photo shoots; (6) Learn French (I have so far completed one beginner lesson with Rosetta Stone!); (7) Draft a handwritten letter to Vanilla Ice and see if he writes back; (8) Work out to Jane Fonda and/or other aerobics videos that were shot in the 70s so that we look fierce in our (9) ironic glamour photo shoots; (10) Play lots and lots of board games...

A week or so after I'd first arrived, the *Wicked* cast celebrated its one-year anniversary of performing in San Francisco. There was a swanky nightclub party and everything, with thumping music and pigs-in-a-blanket-pushing waitresses in skimpy outfits and mini tilted hats. Etai and I, freshly off the proverbial boat, did our best to mingle amongst the cast, oozing charm. All told we were one step closer than strangers and many steps shy of being friends. But we had fun, stuffing our faces and taking awkward Facebook photos. At one point I found myself sitting next to Teal Wicks, our Elphaba at the time, who had distractingly toned arm muscles. Worried that I'd ask for an autograph on a cocktail napkin or squeeze her upper arm, I soon slinked away to the buffet, where I reunited with Etai and loaded up on chicken skewers.

Several days after the party, David Stone, one of *Wicked*'s lead producers, called a company-wide meeting, mandatory for all cast members. Floating on the wind of our one-year triumph, were our wings about to get clipped?

Was it a reprimand? Were we—gasp!—closing? Would the show suddenly be performed by shadow puppets? In my mind, questions abounded.

At the scheduled hour, we all assembled on the empty stage. I sat cross-legged next to Etai, proud to be among the newest cast members of *Wicked*. Front and center stood David Stone, with freshly trimmed salt-and-pepper hair and a neatly pressed polo shirt—decidedly different-looking than I'd been imagining him as one of the mysterious bearded fates of *Wicked*.

Maybe this is just his day disguise, I thought.

The verdict?

Wicked San Francisco would be closing—though not until September. David fielded a quick Q and A about what this would mean for us, and soon we dispersed, the date burned into our minds.

September 5.

It was weird to know our company's expiration date after I'd only just arrived and signed my contract.

To sort things out, Etai and I talked everything over at his apartment while watching *War of the Worlds* and, obviously, massaging each other's shoulders.

"At least it's not some mystery," said Etai, as he started thumping along my spine with violent karate chops.

"Ow!" I yelled.

"Oh, come on, it feels good!"

"Ow!"

"I mean, eight months is a long time—but not long enough to settle."

"Tru-u-u-u-u-ue," I said, through the chopping. "Wo-o-o-ould you qu-i-i-i-it that for o-o-o-o-o-one se-e-e-e-e-c-o-o-o-o-ond."

"Okay, but it's good for you."

Shaking off the pain, I submitted that we should just think of *Wicked* as an eight-month vacation. "It will give me an excuse never to unpack my stuff."

"Good idea," said Etai.

I explained to him that, as far as I was concerned, it was exactly like moving into a college dorm. You knew you were going to leave after two semesters and that people were going to throw up on your floor, so what was the point? (Still, it would be nice to hang that bookstore-bought French print over your bunk.)

Soon we'd switched seats, which meant it was my turn to give Etai his massage comeuppance. On the TV, the aliens had appeared and were slinking around an underground bunker, gangly and disoriented.

"But what I really don't understand," I said, wringing his shoulders, "is how these sickly aliens built those huge tripod spaceships. I mean, they can't even walk straight without freaking out."

"It's true," said Etai, sitting up. "They invented machines with human-evaporating death rays and, look, they're confused by a bicycle wheel."

"Can you imagine them actually building any of their machinery?"

"I can't. Unless one of them is like, 'Hand me the monkey wrench, Beeblethrox,'" said Etai.

I snapped my fingers.

"'Beeblethrox!' That is now the name of my Citizen of Oz character," I said. "I couldn't settle on anything weird enough for that Act I barrel costume, but I think you just nailed it."

"Glad I could help, Beeblethrox."

The takeaways from this conversation:

1) *War of the Worlds* is a flawed film.

2) For a small man, Etai packed a mean karate chop.

3) My ensemble character was thusly dubbed Beeblethrox.

4) With a closing date in sight, there was no easy way to feel settled.

This last one was a biggie. In San Francisco, cast members who had cultivated a life—with apartments, pets, favorite coffee shops—would, in a matter of months, have to kiss those constants goodbye. And then what? In my ensemble days, I wrestled with this paradox of temporariness—of wanting and needing to feel at home, but knowing I was just passing through—over the rainbow and back.

After my promotion to standby, I was presented with a new psychological challenge. With an unpredictable day-to-day schedule, Libby and I lived in a kind of limbo, suspended between two states of extremes. While 5% of our job consisted of high-stakes heart-thumping excitement, 95% consisted of doing absolutely nothing.

You heard me: nothing.

To pass the time, Libby and I had to get creative.

"What should we do today?" she would ask, every single time we met backstage.

"Hmm."

It was a good question. The world was our oyster! Well, the world within five blocks, anyway. We could do anything our hearts desired! Provided we could perform at a moment's notice.

"I guess I could blog?" I would say.

"Or we could do a workout DVD," Libby would reply.

"Or we could start another puzzle?"

"Sounds good. Let's do that."

When I felt a surge of productivity, I kept up with my writing, which had languished when I was busy rehearsing for Elphaba. Other times I would paint, something I used to do a lot in high school. With my mini easel, canvas, acrylics, and brushes I painted Chuck Close-inspired portraits of people's faces, including Kyle the prop guy's baby who, according to first-violinist Cary, had the same name as a 1970s porn star (Taylor Rain).

Now, I respectfully ask that you resist the urge to conclude that getting paid to do nothing was, in fact, awesome. I can see why you might. Heck, before I was standby, that's what I thought, too! But do take a leap of faith with me here—and just believe it when I say that being a standby got to be a bit...much.

There was just.

So much.

Endless...

...waiting!

Libby had been doing *Wicked* for longer than I had, but nothing could prepare either of us for the sudden change of going from nightly ensemble performances to the idle life of a standby. Even worse was the letdown of going from playing Elphaba or Glinda to having to retreat back to the dressing room, our holding cell. There we would wait, separate from the rest of the cast, with a lingering pressure always hanging over our heads.

We weathered long stretches of this schizophrenic limbo: always mostly calm but, under the surface, mildly agitated.

(What's the line from that depressing Emily Dickinson poem? *It goads me, like the goblin bee / That will not state its sting.*)

To cope, Libby and I spent our time chatting on the couch— about our families, favorite fad diets, dating histories. It was essentially like being at a seven month-long slumber party (the kind where you learned the true meaning of over-sharing). We even ordered zebra and leopard print Snuggies online to wear backstage (did you think I was joking?), which helped make the slumber-party experience fully immersive.

To make the space our own, and more cozy, we pinned photos along our vanity mirrors and on the outside of the door, and draped Christmas lights along the "wall" we shared with the female ensemble.

I put quotation marks around the word "wall" because the top of said "wall" didn't actually reach the ceiling, but rather left a two-foot gap that let us hear everything the girls next door were saying. All the chatter, laughter, stereo music, and rise and fall of the show's energy as the girls trickled in and out between scenes came wafting into our space like the delicious smells of a dinner party to which we hadn't been invited. As we listened, we tried to imagine how fun the party must be for everyone who got to go inside: sampling *hors d'oeuvres*, drinking red wine, gossiping about the neighbors.

Occasionally, we would work up the courage to visit. It always began and ended the same: Libby and I would tiptoe in, make a few minutes of small talk, then quickly wrap around through the exit.

Maybe it had to do with the "wall," or the fact that we'd said goodbye to our ensemble days, but for us there was an implicit divide—and that infamous "wall" was a constant reminder: on one side there was a show to do; on the other side was the far-off wish we could join.

Each time, before Libby and I left the girls' room, I couldn't help but cast a look at Alyssa. While training to be Elphaba, she'd taken over my ensemble track—wearing my costumes and wigs, and holding my props. It was like looking at a family portrait to find my face had been scratched out and replaced with a friend of mine's, who was living in my room, playing with my toys, and getting her nose wiped by my mom. I knew it wasn't her fault— no, it was just the way things were.

But if I believed I'd reconciled leaving the ensemble, when I saw Alyssa sitting at my old station I felt a faint, residual sting.

Goblin bee! Buzz off already.

Most nights, Libby and I would don our Snuggies, venture into the hallway, and make visitation rounds to the rest of the cast.

Etai's dressing room was one of our frequent pit stops. He had it all to himself and had decorated the space to look exceedingly masculine, with only a lone gray couch in the center that looked like a deflated elephant. Libby and I would invade this masculine hideaway without knocking and plop down on the elephant, at which point we would usually find Etai in his underwear, working on a crossword puzzle, or wooing various ladies on instant messenger.

Catty-cornered to Etai was French Nic's room. Nic and I had grown closer since he and Marshall had started lifting weights, drinking protein shakes, and reveling in their manly bromance and whatnot. It was fun to pay him pre-show visits, during which we would chat about (1) Marshall, (2) the latest computer technologies, (3) Marshall. We always had a jolly time, and it was not infrequent that during these conversations he would gift me with a free program to upload to my computer. "For to install Photoshop," he would say, Frenchly, handing me a USB cord.

As I downloaded, Nic's stunning girlfriend Neka would often appear, sweeping into the dressing room in some manner of high heel and vintage frock, even if it was minutes before curtain. Neka and I had become sort-of friends during our ensemble days, but many weeks later I still wanted to run, hide, and put on lipstick every time I saw her. Neka was, you see, intimidating: ridiculously pretty, smart, and unafraid to speak her mind. No topic was off-limits—from her opinions of anything, to the trials of being a dancer, to the most personal and otherwise repugnant bodily ailments.

(She and I had actually discussed these bodily ailments while physically onstage, back when I was in the ensemble. Dressed in our elaborate Ozian costumes, in front of thousands of people, our conversations went something like:

FELICIA: Man, I am so bloated.

NEKA: Did you have salty food before the show?

FELICIA: Are corn chips salty?

NEKA: Salt will give you chapped lips, that's for sure. Look at mine, they're shriveled.

FELICIA: I'm constipated.

NEKA: Sometimes when I'm constipated I like to massage my own abdomen, to get things moving.

FELICIA: That is a great idea. Also, what is a yeast infection?)

Next to French Nic was Tom, our Wizard, who was like a more fun version of everybody's uncle. Despite all of his professional success (from *The Birdcage* to *Frasier* to *Heavyweights*), he was not at all aloof in that movie-star kind of way. He usually kept me posted on his latest workout exploits, sometimes going so far as to demonstrate his favorite moves on the carpet (burpees, mountain climbers, jumping jacks) as Libby and I cheered him on.

After completing our rounds, it was back to the drawing board. We'd only wasted 20 minutes. What to do with the remaining 150?

When the dressing room walls got to be too confining, Libby and I would return to our respective apartments, within five blocks of the theater. But things were more tolerable if we stuck together, wallowing in the underwhelming trauma of our shared experience.

During said wallowing I would regress to the college student version of myself, returning to all my favorite procrastinatorial hobbies, like playing Snood or Text Twist, Facebook stalking, or writing rap lyrics that made no sense. Sometimes I would regress as far back as middle school, acting like a possessed freak and scrawling on paper in the secret language I invented in seventh grade—and still use to this day. (I'd made up this language so my friend Kat and I could pass confidential notes in Spanish class. She never learned it, so I was forced to pass notes with myself.)

Even worse was when Libby and I wandered our way to YouTube, keeping tabs on ourselves and various other *Wicked* actresses, falling down the rabbit hole of comparison and competition—which I'd tried so hard to resist.

After these lapses, we would self-flagellate by doing Tracy Anderson workout DVDs—painful not only due to their endless arm and leg raises, but because I found Tracy Anderson to be insufferable.

(Libby would disagree, since to this day she is a sworn Tracy Anderson disciple. But I maintain that her DVDs are the worst! My standby wife and I had many heated debates about this very topic, mid-workout—while Tracy would be like, "This is really good for your body" (instead of giving us actual *cues*)—and I'd be like, "Gee, thanks, Tracy, for being so scientific!"—and Libby would be like, "This woman changed my life! My body is a different body!")

(But I digress.)

When we weren't bickering over Tracy Anderson, sometimes Libby and I would feel inspired to practice our *Wicked* songs. It was important, after all, to maintain the muscle memory required to sing Elphaba and Glinda. The tricky thing about this, however, was that there weren't any soundproof studio spaces—not even the vocal rehearsal room, which itself was surrounded by incomplete "walls."

So, we found the best place to hide was in the women's restroom, belting amongst the stalls in cadence with the live show, whose audio emanated from speakers near the ceiling.

Sometimes we'd switch off, with Libby singing Elphaba and me singing Glinda. Sometimes we'd reminisce about the last time we got to perform together, reenacting certain moments. Sometimes we'd prance around on the tile, dancing with the shower curtains, performing the ensemble routines we used to do onstage every night.

Each time when we were done, we'd erupt into a fit of giggles—so amused that this (the frivolity, the aimlessness, the waiting) was our *job*.

Then, the reality would sink in.

This was our *job*.

And we had many more months to go.

❖   ❖   ❖

Meanwhile, I was rehearsing for another role I'd been cast in: Live-In Girlfriend to Marshall Roy.

So far I'd been learning my part diligently, always showing up to practice prepared—splitting the electric bill, folding laundry, doling out foot rubs. Since Marshall was at first unemployed, we spent a ton of time together; we went to the gym, explored the city, and watched episodes of *No Reservations*, that brash Anthony Bourdain travel show where he would visit Siberia and complain about the cold.

Our own traveling was a bit more circumspect; since Marshall and I didn't have a car, we walked everywhere. But we only made it a mile or two in either direction before our calves and faces started burning—from the rolling hills and skin-slapping wind, respectively. Consequently, the farthest east we ever got was the Ferry Building, a waterfront complex that sold fresh produce, or (in the other direction) the Castro, San Francisco's gay district, where we'd buy chocolate-covered penis cookies.

Indeed, "rehearsing" perfectly summed it up. Under special, once-in-a-lifetime circumstances, we'd taken wildly romantic measures to be together (just like in the movies!). In this way, we were *playing* house: living together, but not *really* living together.

The way we saw it, the stakes were nil. If playtime got to be tiresome, we could blame it on bad timing, or the miserable San Francisco weather, or the fact that there was never a moment in which I didn't look slightly seasick.

No, we wouldn't fall victim to *real* problems—when real life got in the way of relationships. Here in Oz, life itself was so wildly unrecognizable that it was hard to believe anything could have lasting consequences.

Socks on the floor, mold in the grout, spoiled milk in the fridge be damned—playing house was nothing but *fun!*

Oh, sure, there were challenges. For example, I learned that being domestic meant sometimes having to cook—which I almost never did when I lived alone, except when I boiled spaghetti or poured cans of beans into pots and stirred in salt. I successfully hid this fact from Marshall until around the five-month mark. The moment of disillusionment came when I volunteered to make chicken tenders for dinner, and then left them in the oven for two hours. Through each jaw-breaking bite Marshall commented on how "crispy" they were, while I noted that they had the consistency of burnt sand, or rocks.

From then on, Marshall took kitchen matters into his own enormous hands—whipping up meals six or more times a day, each in a matter of minutes.

This was fun for a while. But in order to maintain his muscle mass, Marshall ate close to 4,000 calories a day, or once every ten minutes—which meant not only that the supermarket cashiers knew our first names, but that at any hour of the day there were dirty dishes in the sink.

He just wouldn't stop *eating!*

Even worse were his massive bales of protein, from which he'd scoop his pre-workout shakes. At first I thought them charming, but they grew progressively less so each time I had to leap over them to get to the kitchen sink, or use the toilet, or take out the trash.

Or do anything, really.

Outside our apartment, his Rambo proportions were grounds for celebration.

Inside, they tested my sanity.

I felt like a prisoner in my own home, barred from baseline creature comforts by my clumsy, live-in Hercules.

To avoid conflict, I would try to relax on our patio. There (I thought) I could escape the constant kitchen smells and sounds of clanking stainless steel. But the weather was never above 60 or sunny for more than five minutes, so each short-lived escape ended with me scurrying back indoors—back into the aroma-cloud of roasted sweet potato and baked Brussels sprouts.

Other days, I would try to go for a walk. But inevitably, I would get chased down by the shopping cart lady or her constituents who, in moments, drove me off the streets and back inside.

There I remained: indoors, sitting on the couch, *looking* at the patio (visible through the sliding doors we kept tightly shut to ward away the cold) while Marshall announced he'd be making five pounds of quinoa in the rice cooker.

But, oh, these trials made us *stronger!*

Yes, we became *stronger* when I submitted a verbal treatise on why it was unacceptable for Marshall to leave dirty pans in the sink or use two feet of dental floss with every brushing, or snore so loudly I felt like I was sleeping next to a power tool.

We became *stronger* when Marshall rebutted that I traipsed in mud with my dirty shoes, clogged the drain with my long blonde hairs, and forgot to close the refrigerator anytime I went to get anything.

Yes, this was the stuff of *romance!*

The corrosive, degrading, take-me-back-to-NYC stuff of romance.

In these moments I'd draw a mental map of my Dating History Museum and start planning where exactly I would display Marshall's bust. I'd have to start a new wing for him—the Post-College Collection. In my information pamphlet I'd be sure to mention that we'd had a great run—at first so perfect, then later fractured by circumstance:

When faced with long distance, we couldn't bear to live without each other. Soon, we learned we couldn't live with each other, either.

It was only a matter of time before the spectacular, soul-crushing failure. It had happened with Matt 3.0. Now it was time—time for my next great disappointment.

Another one bites the dust.

But one day, Marshall sat me down on the couch.

"Game plan," he said.

I could see it in his face; he was determined.

"It's just...you're so big," I said.

"I know," he said.

"I'm so bad at being neat."

"You're creative."

"I hate cooking."

"That's okay."

"And you snore so frickin' loudly."

"Okay, so what do we do?"

As we talked, I saw him emerge—that same Marshall who'd been there for me the Week I Didn't Poop, helping me relax and invoking logic through the haze of anxiety. Today, he'd come back stronger than ever, to lead us toward a step-by-step solution.

In his words, when it came to playing house, we'd *committed to the bit*. And nobody was giving up.

So, we brainstormed, finding points of compromise. Marshall would pay for more groceries and I'd take care of the electric bill. He'd buy the floss and sleep on his belly. We'd take turns loading and unloading the dishwasher. He'd store his protein bales under the sink. I'd buy the Drano, take off my shoes, and make a special effort to enjoy our porch while bundled in a winter coat. To mitigate the stress of walking the streets, Marshall would accompany me to and from the theater.

It was slow going: discussions, questions, agreements. But soon, we started to find our way, drafting a Living Together Treaty to help us hold onto our sanity—and, as a result, hold onto each other.

❖   ❖   ❖

"You know, in college, people called me 'Marshall Stewart,' since I baked all the time."

A couple of weeks later, Marshall decided to bake homemade brownies for the cast. I sat on a stool and watched as he fashioned a double boiler to melt bits of baking chocolate into a bowl.

"It's how I show I care," he said.

"The way I show *I* care," I replied, "is that I eat the things you bake."

Per terms of the Treaty, in a clause I'd drafted myself, my new job in the kitchen was not to overcook things, but instead to observe the size and volumetrics of Marshall's muscles as he scooped, stirred, and kneaded. As reward for all of his fine chef's work, I'd even bought him a souvenir *Wicked* apron the day before, which I encouraged him to wear around the kitchen with nothing but underwear.

"Also, can I just say: working out with Nic has really paid off."

Marshall turned on the gas burner, his muscles glistening under the oven light.

"Ha, thanks, you sasser. Would you hand me the spatula?"

I did this as I pitched to Marshall that he should have his own cooking show, called *The Nearly Naked Chef.* "You could cook, while nearly naked," I explained. "Maybe if you wore that apron *Wicked* would sponsor it."

"I told you I would do it," Marshall said as he began stirring the chocolate, "if it involved some kind of badass weapon. Like a sword."

"You could absolutely have a sword, provided you would use it to mince."

Marshall gave me a peck on the cheek. Still stirring, he said,

"So, in the unlikely event *The Nearly Naked Chef* doesn't start until next season, I found some work in the meantime."

"You got the job in Pacific Heights?"

"Yep!"

I whooped and gave him many celebratory butt slaps.

"That's amazing! But did you tell them I was in *Wicked*?"

"I strategized a new approach."

"Brillz! What was it?"

"I said you were an investment banker."

"Ha!" I said, clapping my hands. "I can't think of a job I'd be worse at."

Since arriving, Marshall had been looking for work in San Francisco. But any time he'd landed an interview, he was a near-impossible sell. "My girlfriend's in *Wicked*," he would say—meaning that when the show closed, he'd have to fly the peninsula. But now that I was an *investment banker*, Marshall was set to start work the next day, running the front desk of an upscale health club.

Always a lover of weight lifting and nutrition, Marshall had long been considering a career shift to personal training, and this gym job would be a great stepping-stone for his résumé. As a perk, he could spend slow hours studying for the National Academy of Sports and Medicine exam—laying the bricks for the next stretch of his life path.

"I'm so proud of you," I said, as I walked over and dipped my hand in the baking chocolate. "Mm, scalding and delicious!"

Later that night, we celebrated his new job by feasting on warm "reject" brownies, the broken bits that had stuck to the pan. The chocolate was rich and perfect, the consistency moist yet crumbly.

"You're such a g-unit," I said to Marshall, as he licked his fingers clean. "How are you real?"

He headed over to the sink.

"Oh, c'mon. Now I'm shy."

Marshall washed the pans while, according to the Treaty, it was my turn to load the dishwasher. As I did, I couldn't help but note how lately this whole cohabitation thing had not only become manageable, but was getting to be pretty darn awesome. Marshall was like a live-in, life-size action-figure of many facets: part chef, part personal trainer. Part apron model.

And, of course, part bodyguard.

Eight shows (plus rehearsals) meant Marshall had been carting me back and forth to the theater at least sixteen times per week. Soon he'd befriended each of *Wicked*'s security guards, and after my Elphaba performances would greet me backstage in the dressing room. There, he'd scoop me up in his patented hug/twirl combo, then accompany me to the bathroom, where he'd help scrub the green off the back of my neck. Then we would walk outside, arm in arm, to meet the cluster of audience members waiting by the stage door.

There were families, couples, groups of high schoolers—all eager to stop and chat, and pose the question, "What's it like?" Outside the stage door, Marshall and I had our routine down pat. With my silver Sharpie I signed programs while he conversed with a few *Wicked* regulars—from middle-schooler Joe, who ran my Facebook fan page; to Chris, a Renaissance woman who worked for Major League Baseball and wrangled penguins at the San Francisco Zoo; to Peggy and Dar, a lesbian couple who sent me friendly emails in which they wrote, "hugs to you and the hunkmeister."

I always loved signing autographs and taking photos with *Wicked*'s most diehard fans. Here, I could assign faces to that monolithic void that was the Audience—the black expanse that stretched before me whenever I was onstage. As it emanated laughter and applause—bursts of encouragement—it was like someone saying, *keep going, good job, chin up!*

It was wonderful, in this way, to get the chance later to reply: "Thank you for coming!"

In my many months as standby, these interactions meant the world to me. I even received a bunch of homemade gifts, bestowed in person and in the mail—one of which was a purple t-shirt that featured a picture of my favorite yellow fruit, encircled by the words POWERED BY BANANAS.

Many fans, for whatever reason, looked up to *me*—in all my greenness. I couldn't explain it, but I could understand it: I knew firsthand what a powerful force theater could be—one that struck chords of admiration, aspiration, and gratitude.

I made this wall calendar for you, Mr. Sills!

One *Wicked* regular named Bettie, who'd been a theater patron for decades, took special note of Marshall. "You're quite the boyfriend," she would say to him, under her flat cap. "I always catch you here, outside the stage door."

"Of course I'm here," Marshall said, smiling. "It's my job."

After I'd finish chatting with the fans, he'd assume the position: by my side, ready to take my hand. We'd wave goodbye and together start the journey home—piggyback-ride optional—down Market Street, past our literal next-door neighbors.

"Want me to carry your computer bag?"

"No, thanks, Marsh. I got it."

I smiled.

Sure, the man snored. Sure he ate a small child's weight in cheese and eggs. Sure he used enough floss to weave us a hammock. But this much was true: he always had my back. And the back of my neck.

17. SANGIN' FOR GEENA DAVIS

As Elphaba standby, it was my duty to promote *Wicked* at various San Francisco events. These events could range from parades, to career trade shows, to any number of cultural happenings. It was all bundled in my job of sometimes playing my dream role, sometimes doing nothing, and sometimes singing "The Wizard and I" over a karaoke track.

My first press event was San Francisco's annual Green Festival, "The Nation's Premier Sustainability Event," an exhibition for environmentally conscious brands, products, and consumers. The venue had an appropriately natural feel to it, with huge wooden beams buttressing the ceiling and reaching down to the floor like a tanned giant's legs.

That day I would be the opening act to an eco-friendly fashion show, in which waifish semi-albino girls with paint swirling around their nipples would traipse around to electronica music, all at painstakingly slow speeds. *Wicked*'s PR bit was to have me sing "The Wizard and I" into a handheld microphone with pre-recorded accompaniment. I was more than happy to do this, even though I'm not too keen on handheld mics. My feeling is that they can look either really cool or really lame—a natural extension of the performance, or something that calls attention to the fact that you're *sangin'!*

For me, it's the latter.

As I stood and did my thing (*"the Wizard aaaa naaaa!"*), I could practically feel my head flick, my chin raise, while I grinned like the Cheshire Cat.

All while *sangin'!*

I felt like a mall-pageant talent contestant.

Soon it was over, and I was relieved of my post, at which point I got to mingle with the folks in the audience, a cross section of *Wicked* fans and bystanders who really loved the environment. Underscored by electronica, I commented that from the looks of the semi-albino girls with paint swirling around their nipples, maybe somebody should turn up the heat.

Another press event happened at the Moscone Center, a huge convention complex several blocks from Marshall's and my apartment. As fate would have it, I had come to know this venue in two prior visits to San Francisco. These trips in 2009 bookended a truly magical time in my life when I worked as a marketing associate for medical software (remember, the dreaded day job?).

This magical time—or my "Freshman Year of Life," as I like to call it—spanned those first twelve months out of college when I was trying to be an actor, make money to pay rent, figure out what the heck to do with my English degree, and cut things off with one Matt 3.0, Breaker of Fel's Heart. I was leading a kind of double life, keeping strange work hours and auditioning on lunch breaks. It was, at best, a thrilling Clark Kent/Superman adventure; at worst, an exercise in rejection and living in fear that I was wasting my life—and sacrificing my livelihood for a dream that had all but flickered out.

At the very least, having a day job could distract me. It could distract me from the fact that, without an agent, headshots, or audition appointments, I was failing to take baby steps toward a career. It could distract me from the fact that my checking account hovered at $300.00. It could distract me from noticing that Matt 3.0 had all but dumped me for a French girl in his Parisian host family.

It could distract me from everything. All I had to do was take the F train downtown, ride the elevator up to the eleventh floor, and mouse-click my way to numbness.

It was the best of times, it was the worst of times, as best friend Becky and I used to say.

But really it was just the worst of times.

On the plus side, as marketing associate, I did a lot of writing—the one thing that I loved other than theater. On the not-as-plus side, I was writing things like, "We don't just sell software, we work with you and your staff to achieve your goals!" On the plus side, I kept flexible hours and got free coffee. On the not-as-plus side, I wanted to gouge my eyes out.

Then came the trade shows. This medical software company (let's call it Software, USA—or SUSA for short) would fly me out to the Moscone Center for specialty physician conferences, where it was my job to (1) get people to visit our booth, (2) fend off the advances of horny old businessmen. Through trial and error, I found that the best way to do both tasks was to stand in the aisle and yell, "Software! Get your medical software here!" like a 19th century newsboy, while the CEO, his third commonwealth wife, and my coworker Kate performed software demos on a droning loop.

Together, we four made up almost half of the company, a collection of sweatsuit-wearin', time-wastin', corner-cuttin' individuals who drank, cried, and complained together on a regular basis. This circus of dysfunction was led by its thrice-married ringmaster, or CEO. With his sheet-white beard and mustache he looked exactly like Papa Smurf and, at 10 minutes and 29 seconds, held the world record for Longest Continuous Monologue Ever Delivered to Felicia in a Real-Life Conversation.

Meanwhile, I was living in Queens with a 19 year-old roommate I found on Craigslist who dated approximately 45 men in the span of seven months, half of whom she'd met online, one of whom was a grandfather, and all of whom she'd woo by cooking dinners from a box, whose chicken-y smells I couldn't escape even if I rolled a towel at the base of my bedroom door.

So, you see, those despairing days at SUSA were not all that different from the rest of my life. In that Freshman Year, I felt lost—figuratively and literally, since I would often find myself cabbing through neighborhoods I had never seen before while eating bagel sandwiches, crying, and trying to send international texts to Matt 3.0.

But today, back in the Moscone Center, those days couldn't be further in the past.

Today, I was Elphaba.

I would be singing for a room full of pantsuit-clad ladies who were attending a "women in business" conference. As I waited backstage, cordoned off by curtains, I spotted Geena Davis (of *A League of Their Own* fame) who, as it turned out, had been invited as the event's keynote speaker. We greeted each other with head nods while nibbling strawberries and mini egg salad sandwiches, while I privately noted that she was really tall and Marshall took pictures of her on his camera phone.

When the time came for *sangin'*, my face was projected onto two giant screens on either side of the stage, while below a spider-legged photographer took some action shots. After I held out the final note of "The Wizard and I," I couldn't help but think, *What a funny headline:* "Site of Cruel and Unusual Day Job Becomes Performance Space for Dream Role." It felt like I was taking back all those hours I'd spent imitating Cockney newsboys, or suffocating from the stench of chicken gravy.

As I heard the sound of applause, it hit me: You can never know exactly how everything's going to work out, but in one day—one *moment* even—you can turn things around, and start rebuilding.

LL101: **You have to start somewhere.**

Back in New York, after finally breaking things off with Matt 3.0, I booked my first professional headshot session. From there, I gradually gained momentum. Miraculously, Papa Smurf was supportive. I think he always thought of me as his inept artistic daughter—only occasionally resentful because I didn't know how to build an Excel spreadsheet. But in those later days, he had huge stores of faith in me—even when I had to steal away for auditions, rehearsals, and then finally, when I had to leave to come do *Wicked*. For this, I am grateful. (Thanks, Papa Smurf!)

Now, thanks to determination, a little bit of Luck, and others' support—from my boss, my parents, and best friend Becky—I had changed my life for the better. Now Geena Davis and I were munching the same finger food, while my hunk of a boyfriend stood off to the side, watching, cheering, taking camera-phone photos. I had just performed onstage, representing *Wicked* to the public, and singing a song that, those many weeks ago, I didn't think physically possible.

That day, I couldn't deny it. I was living in Oz, and life was sweet.

❖   ❖   ❖

Still. Every yellow brick road has its speed bumps. It was, for example, impossible for me to get a good haircut in San Francisco. I tried twice, and in both instances requested long layers, angled in the front, please. (I'm not an expert, but I'm pretty sure this is rather standard?) The first stylist cut literally three strands on my head. The second did the opposite, cutting short bangs all the way to my sideburns, giving me a full-on mullet.

The mullet perpetrator had, oddly enough, been recommended by Neka Zang, who (to recap) was so pretty it was disgusting. I think my secret reasoning was that if her stylist cut my hair, I would somehow come back from the appointment with Neka's face. Not only did this not happen, but I had been made to look like a member of the band Whitesnake.

"I don't get it," Neka said as she pranced beside me on a treadmill. "She is such a genius. Whenever she cuts my hair she actually makes it *longer*."

Even though this statement made no sense, I knew better than to question Neka. "Well, even though it looks like a mullet, I guess it does look like a *long* mullet."

I, too, was on a treadmill, doing my best to imitate Neka's every gazelle-like move. In the past few weeks we'd become closer friends. She was still intimidating, but since I'd been witnessing her having to actually sweat to look good, things became more tolerable. (I'm such a great friend, I know.)

"Isn't this so much better than running?" she said, trotting away.

"Definitely," I replied.

"Are you still feeling bloated?" she asked, waving her arms above her head.

"There is never a moment when I *don't* feel bloated," I said, "but I think this will help."

Another speed bump: as standby, it was impossible to stay in shape. While Libby and I could work out in our dressing room, we never knew if during squat number 99 we'd suddenly get called in by stage management for a last-minute swap. Similarly, if I kicked my own butt at the gym in the afternoon, I feared I wouldn't later find the energy to scream, sweat, and wail my way through the Songs of Death.

(Good luck climbing Mount Elphaba when you can barely walk.)

As a compromise, I embraced Neka's innovative trot technique, a low impact, preserve-your-joints workout invented to guard against the repetitive motion of *Wicked*'s dancing. Soon, we were working out at French Nic's apartment building on the regular; galloping, planking, or crunching as Nic and Marshall grunted and clanked heavy things in the corner.

After working out, we'd take the elevator to Nic's apartment funhouse, where the boys would wrestle with Nic's dog Domi (who looked like a much cuter version of a mop) and the girls would discuss the amount of sodium in Neka's microwaveable dinner.

As workout buddies, we killed many birds with one stone:

1) I burned some serious homemade brownie calories in a manner that didn't leave me wrecked.

2) Marshall found manly sanctuary in hanging out with someone not teeming with estrogen.

3) Neka and I admired our respective boyfriends' rippling muscles, as we ignored the homoerotic overtones.

Soon, more than workout buddies, we two pairs were bona fide "couple friends," a Fearsome Foursome that double-dated at lunch or on road trips to Napa Valley, where we sipped wine and ate cheese opinionatedly (imbued—by the transitive property—with Nic's French authority).

Hanging out with Nic and Neka made Marshall and me realize that, in living together, we'd bypassed the simpler pleasures—like double-dating. Now that we were marooned in San Francisco, away from our friends back east, we'd failed to master some of our more basic dating skill-sets. In a sense, our timeline had been scrambled: as a couple, we were eight year-old savants who'd graduated law school—but never learned to fingerpaint.

I explained this to Neka one day as we pranced along, facing each other and holding the treadmill guardrail.

"I don't know how you guys did it," said Neka as she did a spin-pivot pattern on the conveyor belt that blew my mind, "moving in together so soon."

"It's been a learning curve," I said.

"Men. Just look at them," said Neka, nodding over at the boys.

I looked over Neka's girating body to the weight area, where Marshall and Nic were flexing in a bicep-back-muscle-push-up configuration that was too mysterious to understand.

"They're so content to move heavy things up and down," I added.

Through our trotting we delved more deeply into this favored topic of women high on endorphins. Neka, it turned out, had a dating history of adventure and splendor: she'd coupled with musicians, actors, and world travelers, and seemed all the wiser for it.

My dating history was—what's the word? Pathetic?

I revealed to Neka that, through the years, I had meticulously curated my very own Dating History Museum. At her request, I gave her a quick tour.

"Four gay boyfriends?" said Neka. "Was that, like, depressing?"

I explained to Neka how in the emotional aftermath of finding out your boyfriend was gay, you went through several stages of grief. First you felt relieved (his being gay explained why he wanted to watch your videocassette of The Wiz instead of make out). Then you felt pity (the poor kid had to tell his parents he didn't like boobies). Next you felt excitement (you had a new gay best friend, and maybe it would be like a sitcom!). But, in the end, you were left with lasting resentment—for having endured months of feeling unattractive, and questioning what the heck was wrong with you.

Your only takeaway was the scar, puckered and small, from the pinch of the clothespin as he hung you out to dry.

We talked more as I continued the tour, ending things with a recap of Matt 3.0 and our drawn-out breakup.

"How did you know he was seeing the French girl?" asked Neka.

"I read his Facebook messages."

(I'm not too proud of that part, of course; but what if I hadn't? When it comes to catching cheaters, I am a moral relativist.)

During my snoop, at the very top I'd found a day-old message from somebody named Pauline:

"i shiver when i think of last night outrageous sexiness," it said, at which point I considered that the only thing worse than a sexual overture to your boyfriend is when said overture is rendered without punctuation.

"Ouch," said Neka. "Sorry, girl."

We trotted for a few more minutes, and Neka followed up with the question I'd been wondering for months.

"So, how did you know you were ready to date again?"

I looked over at Marshall, who was doing an overhead press with an amount of weight equivalent to a small horse.

Post-heartbreak, I was sure no man would stand a fighting chance. But Marshall had revised everything I'd been taught to think about guys—how they acted, how they treated you. How they looked in aprons.

From there, it had been a whirlwind few months. I'd become a professional actress. I'd moved to San Francisco. I'd played my dream role, many times over. I'd tumbled headfirst into an exhilarating romance.

I thought about Elphaba, and all that I knew about her so far.

She's brave, and sticks her neck out.

"I didn't know," I said. "I just had to wait and see."

It was the truth. You can never know if you're ready. You just have to walk out onto the ledge, and pray that you don't fall.

18. FOUR SHOWS IN TWO DAYS,
OR, IT ALL COMES CRASHING DOWN

Email from Felicia to Esa.

Hey there, Esa!

I really appreciate your support and am so glad you're liking the blog. I do, indeed, know that I'll be going on for all four weekend performances on May 22 and 23 (a Saturday and Sunday), so if you'd like to catch me doing Elphaba, then would be a great time to stop by.

Anyway, thanks for writing, and take care--

All best,
Felicia

As luck would have it, Eden scheduled two vacation days at the end of May. As soon as I heard the news I emailed, texted, g-chatted, and e-carrier-pigeoned everybody on the planet, who within minutes wrote back to say they'd booked their train, plane, and theater tickets.

This was great news.

It was also mildly troubling.

Wicked's summer calendar, you see, meant there were matinee and evening performances on *both* Saturday and Sunday—adding up to four shows in two days. The rest of the cast had been able to adapt to this more grueling schedule, but I'd only done a two-show day once during my first week. I'd have to tackle a four-show weekend as Elphaba cold turkey.

In the weeks leading up to May 22, I went into rehearsal overdrive, revisiting the Songs of Death, over and over. Breathing, belting, clenching. Banana-ing.

A couple of weeks after the news broke, I called my mother to talk plans. It was Tuesday, so I tried my Grandma Yola's house, where my mom paid weekly visits. When there was no answer, I tried my mom's cell.

"Hi, Feleesh!"

"Hey, Mamacita!"

We discussed the upcoming visit—when their flight would get in, where they'd be staying.

"We're so excited for this, we can hardly wait," my mom said.

I explained that I'd been practicing nonstop, hoping to impress our friends and family. I didn't explain, however, just how nervous I was.

"Are you at Grandma's house?" I asked.

"No, actually, I'm at the hospital."

"The hospital?"

"Yes, Grandma was having trouble breathing the other night, so we admitted her over the weekend."

Next, I heard the sound of my grandmother in the background. "Who are you talking to?" she yelled.

"It's Felicia, Ma! Hang on a second."

The phone cut away. I examined my fingernails as I waited, painted the iridescent *Wicked*-issued green that I'd been wearing now for eight weeks straight.

"Why don't you tell your grandmother about your upcoming weekend," my mom finally said. "I know she'd love to hear about it."

She handed over the phone.

"Gram!"

"Hi, sweetie!" Yola's voice blared, as if it needed to project to the other coast all on its own.

"I'm sorry to hear you're in the hospital. How are you feeling?"

"Fine, fine. Your mother tells me you're doing terrific. She saw you in a video, she said?"

"Ha, yeah. She exaggerates. Anyway, I found out I get to play Elphaba four times next weekend!"

"No kidding!"

Somehow, I felt okay telling her: "I'm really, really nervous."

"Oh, you'll do fantastic. I told everyone at the hospital that you're in *Wicked* and how famous you are."

"You are my publicist."

"I'm your grandmother. I'm allowed to brag!"

"I know, Gram."

There was a pause.

"I wish I could visit," I said. "It stinks that I'm so far away."

"You know I would come there if I could," Grandma Yola said. "I haven't missed any one of your shows. Not one!"

"I know, Grandma. But it's okay!"

"It just looks like I won't be able to this time."

"Don't even worry about it for a second," I said, meaning it. "I'm sure there will be many more shows for you to see."

Yola and I chatted a bit more about the drab San Francisco weather, my hunky boyfriend ("your mother showed me a picture!"), and how I'd pay her many visits in the coming fall.

Then we said goodbye, that I'd call again next week, and that we loved each other very much.

❖   ❖   ❖

Expectations were high, and as each day passed I got more and more psyched to tackle a four-show weekend.

But Friday morning, May 21, the feeling was back. The same throat tickle that came to call during my first week as Elphaba—a mossy inclination that could flourish into a bacteria bramble.

This cannot be happening!

Everyone from back east would be arriving that afternoon. Together they'd bought tickets that spanned all four shows. If I missed even one, I'd be letting somebody down. What would they think?

Into the laboratory!

Water, Neti, water, Echinacea tea, water, Neti, water, Vitamin C, water, Umcka, Oscillococcinum, water.

Lather, rinse, repeat.

"Do you want me to prescribe you antibiotics?" my dad asked that night as I greeted him in the hotel lobby, along with my mom and little sister Tessa.

"No, Dad, I need to build up immunity."

"Because I *will* prescribe you antibiotics."

(Parents show their love many ways; my dad showed his through antibiotics.)

(Oh, and snapping photos—but more on that later.)

Together we ate a quick dinner, during which my family told me about their trip ("Logan airport has a great food court"), what they thought of San Francisco so far ("lots of interesting people"), and how excited they were to see me for all four shows ("we got tickets to every one!"). To preserve my throat, I nodded or hand-signaled my replies, all the while rewrapping my nun's habit around my head.

"And you said your agent is coming tomorrow for the matinee?" my mother asked.

I nodded.

"That will be nice to meet her," said my dad.

There was an elephant in the room.

"I don't know if I can do this," I said.

It felt like I was confessing to a crime. The table fell silent.

"Yes, you can," little sister Tessa said, punching my arm. "I saw you on YouTube!"

My family huddled in for a pep talk—like a football team before a play—and they each told me exactly what I needed to do: rest, drink water, take care of myself.

But that's what I've been doing, I wanted to scream.

By the next morning the bramble had only grown thornier.

Damn.

Water, Neti, water, Vitamin C.

I was 50% there. And so many people had come to see me.

Water, Umcka, water.

Gulp.

Banana.

Against my better judgment, I went ahead with the matinee. It was a peculiar performance, to put it lightly; I spent the whole of "The Wizard and I" clearing my throat between notes and hocking up (then promptly swallowing) hard candy-sized loogies of phlegm, which I'd later re-hock and projectile shoot into the offstage trash can. After this, I would drape myself over whatever set piece was closest while Kathleen and Mark blotted my brow and blasted me with a handheld fan, like I was some gimpy green boxer who had all but lost on a TKO.

Whatever you do, don't call out, said my left brain.

Unlike my debut week, calling out had become an option— since as of May 22 Alyssa had completed her Elphaba understudy training.

You should definitely call out, my right brain insisted.

But the thought terrified me.

Here I was, performing for nearly everybody I knew—my family, college friends, childhood buddies, and Ann my agent, who sat in seventh row center with her husband. Had they all traveled 3,000 miles to watch me belly flop into a pool of failure?

Failure! Failure! Failure!

A right-brain chorus sang out, in some weird musical Failure Canon. And the floodgates opened wide.

You're going to embarrass yourself in front of everyone you know.

Quiet.

And then somebody will post it on YouTube.

Seriously—shut up!

As I sat in the dressing room at intermission I remembered all the rumors I'd heard about past Elphabas. These were the *Wicked* urban legends—stories of So-and-So's terrible downfall, whether from polyps, vocal cord hemorrhaging, or other serious injuries that went beyond my novice fears of cracking, forgetting a line, or going slightly flat.

In singing through sickness, was I risking my voice? Would I ever be able to sing again?

Failure! Failure! Failure!

(Shut up, right-brain choirboys! Your lyrics suck!)

Soon, Bryan hustled into the dressing room, adding to the already frenetic mood. The team was busy with my Act II makeup and hair, while I sat quivering like a wet puppy.

"How are you doing, sweetie?" said Bryan.

Dad, you came to my soccer game!

"Not so good," I said.

"Yeah, I can hear it in your voice," he said.

I took a deep breath, then blurted, "I don't think I can do tonight's performance."

Bryan's eyes grew wide, and so did mine, once I knew I'd made a decision without really realizing it.

"Okay, I've got some work to do," he said.

And with that, he dashed out the door. Presumably, he was off to inform Alyssa of the news. As understudy, she was the backup plan's backup plan.

Thank goodness for Edvard Munch.

She was ready just in the nick of time, too, having had her Elphaba put-in the night before. Like me, on the first day she was eligible to play Elphaba, she would have to swoop in and rescue the show.

(**GREEN.** 9. untrained; inexperienced: *a green understudy.*)

Hopefully, she'd brought her pen and paper to take notes on Life Lessons 101, the same lecture I'd heard on that fateful March Tuesday:

LL101: **You can't always plan. The universe may intervene.**

Decision made, I rose from my chair, donning my thirty-pound Act II dress, witch's hat, and shawl. Walking to my post in the wings, I began running "No Good Deed" in my head—knowing it was the last remaining Song of Death. On top of its melody, the Failure Canon played in dissonant counterpoint, so loudly that I wanted to scream.

What was happening?

Here I'd thought I had overcome my fear of failure—only to find that it still sat with me, on my shoulder, whispering (or in some cases, singing) powerful words of discouragement. And amidst the chatter—the cacophony of doubt—one phrase rose loudest, above all the others.

Help me.

At the stage door that afternoon, I saw Marshall, my family, college and childhood friends, and my agent.

"That was killer!" said Ann.

"Thanks for coming," I said as I gave her a hug, silently wishing she'd seen any of the other shows in which I wasn't hocking up loogies every thirty seconds. Next, I turned to Marshall who, without words, scooped me up in his arms and lifted me many feet in the air, twirling me around and giving intermittent squeezes.

Then came my mother. "You're looking at one proud Elphamom," she said as she pulled me in for a full three-minute hug, while my dad snapped photos from all possible angles.

I was grateful for all of the support, but it was totally weird to get praised for a performance that had made me want to crawl inside a hole.

I walked over to greet the fans, signing programs and taking photos. A few *Wicked* regulars had come to the matinee; I'd mentioned something on my blog about the Elphaba dates, and many people had apparently bought tickets.

"A bunch of us are coming back to see you later," a woman in a windbreaker said. "Will you be on tonight?"

"Uh," I looked at Ann, then my mom, then all my friends. I had to fess up. "No, not tonight."

The woman frowned. "Everything okay?"

I pointed to my throat. She nodded in compassion.

"Get some rest, then. And don't worry about it," she said.

I thanked her for the kind words, signed more autographs with my silver Sharpie, and rounded up my family to head down the sidewalk. As we walked from the theater, the toothless coffee-snatching lady appeared out of nowhere and demanded we give her something. My family cowered, while I looked her in the eye and spoke the truth:

"Sorry, my friend. I got nothing."

At the very least, taking off the evening meant I could enjoy a dinner feast with my family. Being of robust Italian descent, my father, Tony Ricci, had long insisted that going to a restaurant should be like a trip back to the Old World. Luckily I knew just the place—a restaurant in North Beach that played Italian movies while you dined.

My parents, little sister, Marshall, and I filed into our seats along a large banquet table, while *Ciao, Professore* played on a flatscreen mounted on the wall. Tacked next to it were strings of garlic and saucepans, while everything else in the vicinity was red, white, or green.

Having lived in Italy, my dad speaks the mother tongue fluently—and never misses an opportunity to do so. Like clockwork, in the first few seconds after sitting down, my dad asked where the waiter was from. And, *molto bene!* He was authentically *Italiano* (accented and all), which was great news for everybody since the quickest way to my father's heart (and a massive tip) was to speak in broken English and later confirm, when asked, that you did indeed *parlare italiano*.

It just so happened that May 22 fell one week after my 24th birthday, so as our waiter went off to fetch San Pellegrino *con gas*, I watched as my family hoisted several tissue paper-filled gift bags onto the table. Enclosed were patterned Victoria's Secret onesie pajamas, and two different versions of an Elphaba doll they had found on the internet. As I dangled the two dolls together, shaking them so they were having a conversation, the waiter exclaimed something in the mother tongue that made him and my dad laugh hysterically. Moments later, the waiter was kneeling by my side.

"This is *Wicked*, yes?" he bellowed, inches from my ear, pointing to one of the Elphaba dolls.

"*Si!*" yelled my father from across the table.

They yelled a bunch of other Italian stuff, after which the waiter put his arm around me and my dad took out his massive paparazzi lens, attacking us with the flash.

"I told him you were the star of *Wicked!*" he said, snapping away maniacally.

"Dad, I'm not the st—"

"Please-a, will-a you please-a sign?" said the waiter, handing me a *Wicked* program. Someone in my family must have chucked him a Playbill in the strobe-light-flashbulb confusion.

"Don't worry," my mother called to me, "we've got lots of extras."

"Good, because I *was* worried," I said.

I still had my silver Sharpie handy, so I inscribed the cover with my signature sign-off, "Wickedly Yours, Felicia Ricci," which I felt wasn't fully appropriate until I added, "*Ciao!*" below it.

The waiter thanked me, bowing his head as he backed up into the kitchen.

"Wasn't he adorable," said my mother.

"Yeah, he was all right," said a teeth-gritting Marshall.

"Don't worry, I only have eyes for gladiators."

"Do you want me to punch him, though?" said Marshall.

"Nah, not this time."

Who were we to punch the waiter? After a year and a half, *Wicked* had become a huge part of the San Francisco theater scene. It was hard to walk a few feet downtown without seeing a *Wicked* ad on the side of a bus, dotting the underground BART stations, or waving on Union Square flagpoles.

After Fossil store guy, I'd been recognized for my job more than I'd expected. It was the *Wicked* effect: once I mentioned that I'd played Elphaba, I was suddenly important in people's minds, worthy of complimentary desserts, bonus spa treatments, or VIP tickets to tourist attractions. I, myself, wasn't a celebrity—but I was *part* of something celebrated—a cultural phenomenon, a chapter in history.

Sure, I was one of its footnotes. But I was there. You just had to look hard.

The waiter reappeared with our heaping plates of gnocchi, pizza, and other carbohydrates. "And a special a-treat for-a the star of *Wicked!*" He walked over and placed a champagne flute before me.

I'm not the star, I wanted to say. I felt my pulse quickening.

AT THIS PERFORMANCE THE ROLE OF ELPHABA WILL BE PLAYED BY FELICIA RICCI.

When standbys went on, their names were displayed on signboards in *Wicked*'s lobby. These signs spelled "once-in-a-lifetime chance" for the cast member—and "certain disappointment" for the audience. If (against all odds) people saw us and liked us, without secretly wishing they could get a partial refund, then bully for everybody. But on the softball team of *Wicked*, the standbys were its benchwarmers.

This wasn't my self-pity talking; this was the painful truth.

In the restaurant, if circumstances had been different, I wouldn't have minded the waiter's special attention. Maybe I would have *liked* basking in the warm glow that *Wicked* cast on me. But that night, it felt less like a glow and more like a spotlight on my shortcomings.

Welcome to the Wonderful World of Wicked.

At the end of the meal, my dad stood once more to capture a final picture-perfect frame: the waiter leaned over my shoulder, and together we toasted my evening of getting sick, as I smiled and pretended to sip the champagne I couldn't actually drink.

I wanted to hide. But like a good actress I sat up straight, struck a pose, and smiled for the camera.

Then, as my dad clicked away, I felt something inside me snap.

On the walk home, Marshall tried to take my hand, but I wriggled it away.

"You okay?"

I picked up my pace, now several strides ahead. I felt the wind bite at my ears, turning icy as it whipped around my hair, which was still damp from my dressing room shower.

"Hey, slow down," he said.

"I'm so sick of this," I said through a stiff jaw.

I saw our apartment's doorway up ahead, so I reached into my bag and scrambled for my keys.

"Sick of what?"

"Everything."

I didn't know who to be mad at. I felt mad at the world. Especially myself.

"Hey, slow down."

"Just leave me alone."

"Fel—"

"Why did you even come here? It's all such a joke."

At this, Marshall stopped walking.

"What are you saying?"

"I hate it here. I hate this stupid street. I hate the stupid green in my hair. I hate that I'm sick. I hate the way my family is making a big deal over the fact that I'm a standby. I hate that we're stuck here. I hate that we're eventually just going to break up anyway—"

"What? What the hell is this? Calm down," Marshall said.

"Seriously, leave me the alone. *Go away!*"

I turned the key and headed inside. At the top of the stairs, I could barely catch my breath and felt my heartbeat pounding in my throat. I threw down my bag and shut myself in the bathroom, drawing a hot bath.

There I lay, with my chest covered in Vapo Rub. I watched heavy mist fill the room—a rainforest with a shower curtain. I sank down into the water until my head was submerged beneath the suds. The warm pressure seeped around me; into my ears, against my eyelids.

Then it hit me: this was the feeling I'd been having for months. Despite my triumphs, ever since I'd taken on the role of Elphaba I couldn't escape the feeling that I was underwater; surrounded on all sides by preoccupations and anxieties, with no easy way to gasp for air.

And the person holding my head underwater? It was me.

My own worst enemy.

I exhaled, feeling a cascade of bubbles along my face.

After breaking the skin of the water, I wiped my eyes and saw Marshall sitting next to me on the bathroom tile.

"Hey," he said.

"Hey."

"You okay?"

"I'm not sure."

"Look. Don't beat yourself up. I mean, four shows in two days? That's ridiculous. Plus, the pressure of having everyone here—"

"I thought my first time on as Elphaba was supposed to be the hardest. Or the Week I Didn't Poop."

"Well, they're all tied, I think."

"When will it get easier? I just want it to get easier," I said.

"Give your body some time to heal and catch up."

"But what if I have to call out tomorrow?"

"Then you'll call out."

"What if—" I felt my throat catch. It always did that whenever I was about to say something scary. "What if this isn't right for me?"

"What do you mean?" asked Marshall.

"Theater. *Wicked*. What if it's not for me."

Saying it felt like giving away the ending to the movie of my life, the one I'd invested 24 years in watching. Months before, it had been a romantic comedy. Lately, the third act had taken a turn towards melodrama.

"Then you'll figure it out," said Marshall.

"I don't know what I want sometimes," I said, mad at the screenwriters for robbing me of my confidence.

"That's okay, Fel," Marshall said simply.

"But—" I stopped mid-sentence, slapping my palms down onto the water with a *clap*, "I don't know what to do.

"It's okay," said Marshall. "Everybody feels that way sometimes."

"Not true," I said, sniffling.

I looked at Marshall. In the humidity, his sideburns had curled up around his ears and beads of mist were forming over his brow. The bathroom felt like a furnace. But still, he stayed.

"Where did you just go?" I asked.

"I stopped by the bodega. We're out of Vitamin C, so I thought I'd pick you up some orange juice."

"Oh, Marsh," I said, tears in my eyes.

Forget carb-sweet-fat baskets. At that moment, orange juice was the most romantic gift I'd ever gotten.

I wanted to take back our walk home—or for that matter, the last few weeks. Since I'd begun my self-defeating quest for excellence, I'd become even more engrossed in my work. Gearing up for May 22, I'd been disregarding some of the Treaty terms, doing everything in service of my voice, my health, my goal. Meanwhile, Marshall was keeping absurd hours, walking me home from the theater late at night, cooking midnight dinners of poached eggs on toast, then rising a couple of hours later to open the health club at 5:15 a.m.

Through it all, he hadn't complained. He hadn't called me names, or told me I was selfish. He'd been there—just as he always had. On the bathroom floor, through the humidity, the pressure, the trauma, the auditions, the callbacks, the cross-continental moves. He was always at the ready with piggyback rides, oatmeal raisin cookies, orange juice, and encouragement.

He was Marshall Roy. So profoundly different from anyone I'd ever known.

And here I was, screwing everything up.

"I'm sorry," I said.

"For what?"

"For everything. For having you come all the way to San Francisco to be with me, and then watch me act like a totally psycho person." I flicked some water with my index finger and thumb. "I'm sorry."

"Apology *not* accepted," said Marshall, leaning in, "because you have nothing to apologize for."

"Not even for being totally mean?"

"I'll let you have a free pass tonight."

"Oh, Marsh."

"The thing is," he said, hugging his knees to his chest, "I'm always in your sidecar."

"You are? Still?"

"Fel. Do you even have to ask?"

When we'd first faced the possibility of a long distance relationship, we came up with this idea of a "sidecar." Whenever one of us went on a journey, we said, the other would be there—through bumps, detours, or traffic jams. The meaning kept evolving, but this much we knew: if we couldn't be there physically, we'd be there emotionally. Invested, present, forging ahead.

As life unfolded, we'd keep switching off who was in the driver's seat. No matter the route, together we'd press on.

"Nothing can stop us," I said.

"You got it, buddy."

"But, okay," I said, sitting up through the suds, "how do I get better?"

I gripped the sides of my neck, pressing my swollen glands.

"If you can't do the shows tomorrow, that's totally fine. No matter what, you've done it—more than you ever thought possible. I mean, you got promoted in two weeks! You went on as Elphaba mid-show, your first day on the job! You survived the Week You Didn't Poop!"

"And what is worse than not pooping?"

"You did two shows your second day, then later while you were sick!"

I laughed as Marshall stood at full, towering height, waving his fist for emphasis. "You're Elphaba Thropp, for God's sake!"

Elphaba Thropp, brave and uncompromising.

The next day I woke up and swallowed. Gloom and doom be damned.

I think I can do this.

I rolled over, grabbed my phone, and texted David.

❖   ❖   ❖

And so the world didn't end.

(LL101: **Surprise, surprise.**)

The weekend came and went, though not exactly as I'd hoped. No, I hadn't done perfectly, but I'd done my best—squeaking in three performances in two days.

Since the show must go on, one person's falter became another's triumph, and Alyssa made an amazing Elphaba debut. Days later, the world's most efficient bootlegger struck again—posting the end of her "Defying Gravity" for the eager masses.

Ah, the great circle of life.

My family flew out of town early that Monday morning. Marshall was on duty at the gym, so I took the whole afternoon to recoup, doing my usual routine of Neti Potting, gargling hydrogen peroxide, drinking my weight in water, and plopping down on the couch to watch *Say Yes to the Dress* (the most repetitive yet inexplicably entertaining TV show ever made).

As suspense built over whether Tammy would find the perfect mermaid silhouette in her price range, I got a call from best friend Becky.

"Hello, son!"

"Son!"

"What's up, son?"

"Son, how was your Elphaba weekend?" Becky asked.

I recapped the minor drama of my calling out, taking special care to reenact the Flashbulb Feast, Italian accents and all.

"Fel, you are the best. Three shows in two days? That is insane."

"Are you going for a run?" I asked, since her voice was cutting in and out.

"I'm doing the Pilates 100 while you're on speaker."

"Oh, amazing," I said.

"So, changing the subject," Becky panted, "guess who I ran into this week."

"Who?"

From the sound of her voice, I already knew.

"Matt 3.0.—in the flesh!"

And here I had buried him in my Museum mausoleum, only to find he had quietly escaped to haunt the streets of Manhattan.

"Did you talk to him?" I asked.

"Yeah! And it was super awk."

According to Becky, on St. Mark's Place in New York's East Village she had exchanged ten sentences with one Matt 3.0, Breaker of Fel's Heart, who, according to official testimony, had "looked unattractive" and was wearing a hemp bracelet—a huge fashion faux pas for any man in Becky's book.

"Don't worry though," Becky said. "I told him you were living with a fitness model."

"What?"

"Marshall *has* shot fitness ads."

(It was true. He had.)

"How are things with Marshall, by the way?"

Ugh. I hated talking about Marshall and Matt 3.0 in the same conversation.

"Things are good," I said, hesitating. I took a breath and told Becky about the senseless fight we'd had two nights before—about how Marshall's and my lovesick haze had at first been unassailable, but had been tested by our living together, then lately by the stressors of *Wicked*.

"Fel, you're incredibly stressed—"

"I know, I know," I said. "Still..."

My voice trailed off. "I guess everything is going to be okay."

"Fel, don't sweat it," said Becky. "I feel good about things as long as you can talk critically about what's going on. That hasn't always been the case with you, right?"

Becky had a point. While dating Matt 3.0 I had been unable to see things as they really were. Whatever the reason, I ignored all the red flags and kept going, full speed ahead—with my head down and my heart on my sleeve.

"You're sure he looked unattractive?" I asked.

"Oh, absolutely; like a post-op Michael Jackson."

"Still, I'm weirded out," I said. "I feel like this is a bad omen."

"It is definitely not an omen," Becky said. "But if it is, the only thing it's predicting is many more years of Matt looking terrible and wearing man jewelry."

Laughing, I tried to seize control of my imagination. If the ghost of Matt 3.0 was stalking the streets, I couldn't let him weasel his way into my thoughts, confidence, or relationship with Marshall. Instead, I would visualize him worming back through the mouth of his mausoleum, where its stone door would close behind him, sealing itself shut, sturdy and cold.

Right before Becky hung up, she added (almost telepathically), "Don't worry. You and Marshall are *not* you and Matt."

That afternoon, my Gentle Rambo came home from work with my belated birthday gift: a bouquet of flowers and a dinner invitation to Gary Denko, one of San Francisco's best restaurants.

"I wanted to wait until the stress of your weekend was over," he said, "so you could enjoy it."

We donned our evening best and cabbed over, where we spent two hours indulging in medium-rare meats, sparkling wine (special occasion permitting), and cheeses (that we selected off a bona fide cheese cart). Marshall had gotten the restaurant recommendation from French Nic, who'd put in a good word with his hostess friend. This meant we got the dimly lit corner booth, replete with sequined pillows, *amuse-bouches*, and a complimentary dessert.

As we alternated decadent bites and puckered kisses, I was reminded of my early days with Marshall—when in spite of all his good qualities I still expected to see him plastered on the nightly news, branded a heart-and-banana-stealing convict. I thought of our first meeting at Serendipity, then of his oatmeal cookie surprise, then when the French woman prophesized our love as we ate chocolate cake. It had been a charmed beginning.

Since then, we had weathered unprecedented circumstances. As I'd told Neka, our "relationship steps" had been shuffled in San Francisco.

But that was our story—and so far, it had worked.

As Marshall smiled at me (candlelit, with tousled hair and wrinkled shirt collar) I knew in my heart that rules, relationship steps, and circumstances really didn't matter. Love didn't have a location or storyline.

Love was anywhere.

It was here, in the back corner of Gary Denko; at home, in fuzzy bathrobes; in airports, saying goodbye over shared muffins; in little yellow envelopes left on bathroom mirrors. Our backdrops kept changing, but together we stayed strong.

After dinner, Marshall and I rode back on an old-fashioned trolley car. As we picked up speed, I stood in the rear under the open sky. We sailed over the hills, the horizon raising and lowering with each dip and crest, while I felt the insistent wind against the side of my face.

The memory returned.

Matt 3.0 and I had broken up, over and over. Each time, I thought we'd get another chance—mostly because I couldn't accept our truly fantastic failure. The kind of failure that washes over you and leaves you feeling drenched for weeks, months, even years afterward.

It's time, Fel.

After our third or fourth breakup, there I was in Central Park, standing on the huge, jagged rocks. I put on my headphones and began listening to a very important song.

Time to defy gravity.

It was a song that had stirred me the very first time I heard it, as that surly and disbelieving English major, evolving her idea of a dream. The song cycled back throughout my life, many times: on my first solo trip to NYC (iPod, Metro-North), after sealing the envelope that contained my senior thesis (Bose speakers, dorm room), then later while auditioning for my dream role (piano accompaniment, neon green casting office).

After those final belted notes of "Defying Gravity" during my *Wicked* audition, I had started to cry. At the time, I hadn't understood it. Was it nerves? Was it stress? Or: was I circling around a memory?

Julie had told me to recall something emotional. Somehow, what I thought I'd buried deep had boiled up to the surface. Each time I'd performed in San Francisco, the memory must have churned—of our final breakup on that windy day in Central Park, those many months ago.

As Elphaba, I could face the feeling of loss. But could I face it as me?

Closing my eyes, I stepped out to the edge of the trolley car and lifted my head. The wind, in its speed and chaos, tore at my hair; strands slapped against my chin and neck as the car dove through San Francisco's valleys.

It's over.

Our speed had picked up, but I kept my eyes sealed tight, waiting for something.

Never contact me again.

All the hurt, the pain, the regret that still lingered—it was time to let go.

Goodbye, forever.

Soon, the trolley came to a stop, and the air was still. I opened my eyes and sighed, then said out loud:

"See ya."

Matt 3.0 wasn't a ghost. He wasn't an enemy. And he wasn't Marshall.

He was a memory—nothing more.

And I had to stop being afraid.

Hopping off of the trolley, Marshall stepped toward me with an outstretched hand. Arm in arm, we walked, our shadows long and gangly from the low-hanging sun.

"Marsh," I said.

"Yeah, Fel?"

I love you, I wanted to say. Instead, I pointed forward.

"Look."

Our shadows were like liquid, flowing across the sidewalk as we pressed on.

"You look like Gumby," he said.

As we turned the corner, the shadows danced with us, glued to the bottoms of our feet. Soon they began to shrink, until they were fat and foreshortened. Compared to Marshall's, mine was shorter still, but met his in the center where our arms were linked.

"Looks like I'm in a sidecar," I said.

"It does," said Marshall.

This time I said it out loud.

"I love you."

Failure had become opportunity. I'd met Marshall, gotten cast in my dream role, and moved to San Francisco. The difficulties came and went, but now I had a better understanding of what to do—and how to let go.

Over a year later, in the Land of Oz, it was all starting to make sense.

(LL101: **You can overcome any challenge. No matter what.**)

Little did I know, my biggest challenge was waiting around the corner.

❖   ❖   ❖

After my family's visit, Eden told me she'd be taking another weekend off in a mere two weeks. This meant I'd get another shot at tackling four shows in two days.

Maybe I can redeem myself?

Once the news was official, I dialed my mom's cell. She told me she was at the hospital. Yola had been readmitted with more breathing problems and, most recently, abdominal pain.

"Is she okay?"

"She's been on and off," said my mother. "But you know your grandmother—feisty as ever."

It was true. My grandma had fended off sickness for years. In her checkered love story with disease, neither could commit or let the other go.

If anyone was going to give in, it wasn't Grandma Yola.

She was a warrior in a senior-citizen disguise, surviving the untimely death of her husband (my grandfather) almost two decades ago, then withstanding hypertension, joint pain, and a recent two-year battle with lung cancer—which, of course, she banished into remission.

My mom explained over the phone that, despite the setbacks, Grandma Yola was gearing up for my cousin's wedding that weekend; she absolutely refused to miss it, even if it meant being rolled in with an oxygen tank. Yes, wheelchair be damned—she'd be dressed to the nines (as always) in her freshly pressed, shimmery gold suit, with her hair impeccably coifed.

No, it wouldn't be a wedding without her. Grandma Yola was an institution, a fixture at any family event—not just in her later life, but through all the years I knew her growing up. She was a steady constant—a homemade-pizza-wielding, advice-dispensing, opinion-thrusting spitfire who taught me about painting, balancing a checkbook, and protecting my favorite books with brown parcel paper.

She came to all my shows—the first to cheer, the last to stop clapping, the first to turn to her neighbor to boast, "That's my granddaughter," and the last to apologize for it.

"Maybe you should talk to her," my mother said into the phone. "Make sure you talk to her," she repeated.

"Hey, Gram," I said.

"Hey, doll," said Yola. Her breathing was heavy.

"I hear you're going to Erika's wedding? That's exciting." I hated myself for sounding chipper.

"Oh, I wouldn't miss it," she said. "And I won't miss *Wicked*."

After the cancer, her health had grown more fragile, but still she was the same Yola. The Yola who would stand up against anything. The Yola who was proud of her family, of her strengths, and of proving, time and again, that she was right. Nothing—not even sickness—could stop her.

"Listen, Gram, I miss you a lot. And when I go on as Elphaba next week, I'm going to be thinking about you the whole time."

"I'm so proud of you," she said.

The following Thursday, I was on an escalator. Marshall was to my left. We had just gotten off the BART train, and were heading up to the mall for a special face wash I just had to have. A woman in front of us was wearing a black and orange San Francisco Giants jacket and stood next to a young boy in a sweatshirt.

Funny how you remember the small, stupid things.

The woman was petite, much too tiny for her sports jacket. The Giants were having a strong season, finishing May with five out of seven wins. The city had been giddy from the excitement. I stared at the block letters, GIANTS, in garish Halloween colors, as my phone started ringing in my jeans pocket.

"Hello? Mom?"

That Sunday night I stood in the dressing room shower, tears blending in with the stream of water that poured down my face. After Marshall helped scrub off the last bit of green, we met a car outside the theater, headed to the airport, and flew to Rhode Island to bury my grandmother.

I had accomplished my goal: four shows in two days. But I didn't care.

I just wanted my grandma back.

❖   ❖   ❖

Coming home, black-and-white Kansas was awash with color. Siblings, parents, and cousins were there to hug, swap stories about my grandmother, and inquire about the bits of green around my ears. It was the bitterest of sweets: returning to a place you loved, to say goodbye to someone who had defined that place for you.

In this way, home felt changed. Like I'd skipped out on someone and come back to find they'd dyed and cut their hair, or put on a fake nose with glasses. I regretted that it took my grandma's dying to get me to come back.

Why hadn't I been there to say goodbye? (Not over the phone, but in person?) Why hadn't I been at my cousin's wedding to compliment my grandmother's hair and shimmery gold suit? If I'd known what the year would bring, would I have gone off to do *Wicked*?

Back in San Francisco after the funeral, I felt so confused. Before each performance, covered in green, not only could I not recognize myself, but I could barely look in the mirror.

Watching the sunrise on my patio after one sleepless night, I called my mom.

"I miss Grandma," I said through tears.

"Me, too," she said with a sigh.

We talked and cried, and I told her how my head felt clouded by doubt.

"I don't know why I'm back here," I said. "I guess coming home got me questioning again. Asking myself what to do once *Wicked* is over."

"Take it one day at a time," my mother said.

"I hate being so far away now. There's just so much I want to do."

"The joy is in the journey," my mom replied, something she said to me often.

We talked some more about my grandma, and about how beautiful the funeral had been. Soon, we'd reached that place of emptiness—where we'd dumped out everything and had no more energy. All we could do was try to breathe.

After a silence, my mother spoke.

"If you think about it, Felicia," she said, "your grandmother knew you only had a certain number of Elphaba shows. I'll bet she just had to find a way to see you last weekend."

"Ha. You're right." I hadn't thought of this. "And I wouldn't put it past her, you know?"

"She was with you," said my mom, "I'm sure of it."

"You think?"

"Of course she was. And you know what? She's going to brag about it from now until the end of time."

19. SAYING GOODBYE

The countdown to closing began.

After my grandmother's funeral, I slowly began to mop myself off the floor. Instead of dwelling in sadness, I tried to approach the final months with optimism, working to table my feelings of guilt or needling dread about what the heck I was going to do come September.

In June, Eden—the idol and mentor—announced she would bid the cast farewell, and that a to-be-determined replacement actress would fill in through September.

In the face of this news, it occurred to me that I hadn't, as planned, become Eden's loyal protégé. It had been trickier than I thought for a standby to get to know her principal actor—let alone kiss her ring and lounge with her in togas on large rocks. But that was the nature of it: Eden always worked when I didn't, and vice versa. Determined to do something about it, I emailed Eden and asked her to meet me for lunch.

A couple of days later and there we sat, an Elphaba and her standby, at a table in an outdoor garden, tying up loose ends over chicken curry.

"This place is great," Eden said, as she took a bite from her sandwich, her green nails standing out against the white ciabatta bread.

"Thanks again for meeting me," I said, talking like there was dust in my mouth. (Although I'd known her for a few months now, I still felt like a stammering theater geek.)

"No problem, Felicia—my pleasure."

With permission to proceed, I sprung into action, asking Eden about her vocal health rituals, what it had been like standing by for Idina Menzel or originating the title role in *BKLYN*—the burning questions I wouldn't ever have the chance to ask again.

"And how about your *Wicked* audition?" I asked. "What did you do to prepare?"

Eden told me she'd been coached by Stephanie J. Block, a former Elphaba who'd played the role in *Wicked*'s first workshop.

"And, man," she said, "am I glad I had Stephanie. I could not act at *all* back then."

"You've got to be joking," I replied. "*You?*"

Everybody knew that one of the reasons Eden was such a phenomenal Elphaba was not just because of her voice, but because of her captivating acting.

"No, seriously, I had no idea what I was doing. Singing, I could do. But acting? I had to work at it—really hard."

As we laughed together, I felt myself growing more comfortable. It was so easy to talk to Eden. She was frank and honest, and as she reminisced she leaned her head back, looking up at the trees.

"And I remember," she said, "I had to go on the night after Idina won the Tony." She laughed to herself and shook her head. "Talk about having to win over a disappointed crowd."

Eden, like me, had been a standby. I loved this fact. While it was years in her past, she had at one point known what it felt like to be in limbo, with the burden of having to prove herself, time and again.

Being standby had first bonded me to Libby. Now, I realized, it also bonded me to Eden. At lunch, we lamented our strange Elphaba fate of always looking slightly off-color and never *quite* being able to wash away all the green. Soon we were two girls gabbing away—about mishaps, relationships, her life in L.A., and what it had been like having to do long distance with her soon-to-be husband. As she saw it, they would make anything work.

"Joseph," she said, "was the first man who took precedence over work. That was huge for me."

I told Eden about my own adventure with Marshall—how what had begun as a romantic comedy premise lately evolved into something much more real and lasting, in that scary life-changing way.

"When you know, you just know," she said, smiling.

"Not to kill the tender mood or anything, but..."

I pulled out my Blackberry and showed her a picture of Marshall, shirtless.

"Girl," she said, laughing, "you've got to keep this one, if only for his abs."

Since first trailing Eden, I'd known her to be a generous spirit; at lunch I was reminded of this once again. Despite her fame, she took extra care to stop and take notice of others. To be there for somebody like me.

Somebody *green*.

But I suppose, at the end of the day, we had that in common. Eden's complexion was light like mine, tinted ever-so-slightly from remnants of makeup. She wore a crocheted hat over her rich black hair, which hung in waves down below her shoulders—an accessory that was as stylish as it was practical.

"Whatever hides the green," she said, smirking.

This reminded me of one last topic.

Should I bring it up?

It was an anecdote from my past that I'd nearly forgotten. But I had a hunch Eden would understand.

"I haven't told anybody this," I said as I furrowed my brow, "but one time this director randomly paused rehearsal and told me I needed to look better. Like, prettier. Actually, his exact words were, 'You know, you could look really pretty if you just tried.'"

"What, was he nuts?"

I laid down the facts.

"I mean, I always look nice for auditions and stuff," I said, "but sometimes, at rehearsals...I don't know. It's just not 'me' to always look *perfect*. Have you ever felt that the business puts pressure on you?"

"You're preaching to the choir," Eden said as she leaned in. "Okay, on the one hand, I get it. This is a looks-based business. But at the same time, it's like: a girl can only do so much." She took off her crocheted hat and ran her fingers along her hairline. "I mean, look at this."

"I feel your pain," I said, in green girl solidarity.

"There are some people who are always going to look perfect. They're going to come out of the stage door looking totally fabulous—like Shoshana. After her shows, she would appear in full makeup, and dark glasses, looking totally fierce. Me? I don't have the energy."

She paused, then looked me in the eye. "You just have to be yourself."

After the last shred of chicken curry disappeared from our plates, we paid the check, hugged, and parted ways down the sidewalk.

As I walked, I felt a spring in my step.

I just had lunch with Eden Espinosa!

The 12 year-old me would not have believed me if I told her.

Rounding the corner, I realized it was obvious: the reason Eden was so astounding was not because of dressing room rituals, resume credits, or hundreds of thousands of fans.

It was because she was so very *human*.

❖ ❖ ❖

All around, *Wicked*'s tectonic plates were shifting. On the same day Eden was scheduled to leave, Kendra (our Glinda) and French Nic would also bid the cast farewell—Kendra to perform in a new L.A. show, and Nic to star as Bert in the touring company of *Mary Poppins*.

Marshall and I were thrilled for him, but as the most enduringly peppy Fearsome Foursome member whose energy level rivaled even that of his mop-like dog, Nic would be sorely missed.

To ring in his last few days, the Fearsome Foursome met on Monday for one last workout session, during which there was much trotting (the girls), homoerotic grunting (the boys), and wistful reminiscing (everybody).

"I don't know what I'll do with a new Fiyero," I said to Nic.

"How will any of us cope," said Marshall, who was definitely more upset than I was.

"Bert is a great role and everything," I went on, "but I'm positive you'll miss getting your face smeared with green during 'As Long As You're Mine.'"

"Oh, no doubt," said Nic.

Post-workout, the four of us took the elevator to Nic's apartment, where we squared things away, cleaning the floors and surfaces while episodes of *Family Guy* played on Nic's flatscreen. As a thank-you, Nic gave Marshall and me a gift card to a wine shop, and every last one of his Costco-bought toilet paper rolls, which numbered 28.

"This is seriously the best gift ever," Marshall said. I thought he meant the wine card, but then saw he was lifting the shrink-wrapped toilet paper in his arms. As both a lover of a good bargain and a person of epic proportions, Costco was like Marshall's Disneyland, what with its 70-packs of chicken wings and swimming-pool jars of mayonnaise.

He looked over at me, grinning. "Our butts are going to stay so clean."

Soon the space was mostly empty, with a few lingering electrical cords and pieces of furniture. It dawned on me that Nic's apartment had been the site of the very first cast game night. Etai had been dog-sitting for Nic when the rest of us had invited ourselves over, eating Nic's tortilla chips, playing his Xbox, and talking to his dog in Sean Connery voices while Chris Hansen brought truth and moral justice to America.

Time flies, my clichéd interior monologue thought, as I emptied a dog hair-filled dustpan into the trash.

An hour later, we were saying our goodbyes, heading through the doorway as Nic's mop dog barked us a farewell.

"I'm going to miss that guy," said Marshall as we walked onto the elevator.

"Me, too."

In the coming weeks, several more of *Wicked*'s cast members left to take jobs in new or long-running shows, while replacements flew in for the remainder of the run. By mid-summer, the cast I had once known was nearly half gone. Even conductor Bryan took his leave, off to music direct *Next to Normal* on tour.

"Thank you for everything," I told him after his final show.

"I'm so proud of you," he said, simply.

As we hugged, I realized that while Bryan had started out as my distant, power suit-wearing dad, we were saying goodbye as friends. Months later, he would confide in me that the reason he'd pushed me so hard was not because of some evil music director vendetta—but because he had believed so strongly in me. He had known, even before I did, that I could climb Mount Elphaba.

Among our new cast members were Alli, our Glinda, and Marcie, who had played Elphaba on one of the national tours. Like Eden, Marcie ended up calling out once or twice a week, which meant a bunch more bananas and note sessions with David.

Alli, on the other hand, never called out. Not once. Consequently, Libby descended into new depths of boredom, denial, and eventual acceptance of the fact that she would never again play Glinda in San Francisco.

"Just wait it out, Libby," I told her, knowing how stir-crazy she must have become. "You're almost there."

September 5.

It loomed ahead, like a storm. A cyclone, even. One that would sweep everyone home, and leave *Wicked* behind.

In these final days, it was strange to keep going while knowing the rug was about to be pulled from under our feet.

Or maybe it was like the rug had already begun to roll, a few inches each day, as *Wicked*'s apparatus started to deconstruct. Storage boxes appeared, and handouts were taken down from the bulletin board, replaced by other handouts about how to prepare for the final weeks. Soon enough, the sets, props, costumes, paper cups, plastic spoons, and dressing room tchotchkes would all be gone.

Where would they go?

I couldn't help but imagine everything getting dumped into crates, carted away, then left somewhere in a warehouse, like that final shot in *Raiders of the Lost Ark*.

Poof!

Forgotten, in a blink.

In my mind, there was still so much to be done. For example, Libby and I had yet to film and edit a full-length workout video, set to discotheque-inspired *Wicked* remixes. Etai and I weren't even close to finishing his entire film collection—which was, according to him, the definitive filmography of modern cinema. I hadn't gotten to hang out with the ensemble girls as much as I'd hoped, due partly to my own persistent shyness and the invisible force of the "wall."

And I hadn't decided what the heck to do once I got back to New York.

Libby and I discussed these End of Days matters in our dressing room as we scrambled to finish our final puzzle project. It was a full-sized *Wicked* poster—that same iconic image of Glinda whispering into Elphaba's ear. Libby's plan was to complete it, have everybody sign it, shellac it, and frame it for her bedroom.

"You're so conscientious," I said to Libby. "Nobody even signed my high school yearbook."

"It'll be a fun keepsake," she said.

Also helping with the puzzle was first-violinist Cary from game night, who visited our standby dressing room at every intermission. He was a true puzzle whiz—somehow able to distinguish all-black pieces from other all-black pieces. To do this, he painstakingly categorized each piece by how many holes or pegs it had, placing it in the appropriate row and column, with all the pieces facing the same direction. It was neurotic, but genius— since before that our puzzle-building technique consisted of me shouting things like,

"I think I found the piece that looks like a whale!"

Only three weeks from closing night, and the puzzle was nearly complete, with one or two patches missing around the border.

"Go on without me, ladies," Cary said, "I have to get back to the pit."

"We won't finish until you come back!" Libby called to him as he made his noble exit.

"The hell we won't," I said. "This puzzle is the bane of my existence."

Yes, the puzzle was our final dressing-room frontier. Excepting our *Wicked* remix workout video, we'd exhausted all activity options. We'd even done a "Witch Switch," wherein we donned each other's Elphaba and Glinda costumes and wigs, while I painted Libby green and she bedazzled me in pink makeup.

But those days were behind us, and the puzzle was our last great push to the end. It was time to make something of this whole experience. All we had to do was assemble those last few pieces.

"Have you found an apartment in New York yet?" I asked Libby as she got on her hands and knees to look under the couch.

"A lot of people are telling me to sublet, in case I have to go on a tour or something."

"Good idea."

"What about you? Ah! Found it." Libby climbed back up holding an all-black puzzle piece in her hand.

I explained to Libby that I still had my Hell's Kitchen studio and Marshall still had his Brooklyn one bedroom. The official word was that we wouldn't combine forces. But secretly, I hoped we would.

Libby and I talked more about what life would be like back in New York. We'd be unemployed, this much we knew. No paycheck. No certainty.

"No matter what, we'll be in New York," Libby said, ever the optimist, "where everything happens."

"It's true. Anything is possible."

I looked at Libby as she pored over Cary's puzzle-piece grid. I had never known anybody like her. Despite our differences, we related to each other so well.

"I'm going to miss you, obvs," I said.

"Obvs!"

"In New York, we'll just have to have actual slumber parties."

"And do a million workout DVDs."

"Oh, I am never doing Tracy Anderson again."

"She changes lives!"

As we bickered like the married couple we had become, it occurred to me that "New York" was our stand-in for "scary, impossible-to-predict future."

Once we flew back, who knew what would happen?

New York.

It was anybody's guess. But knowing Libby would be there made everything seem ever-so-slightly better.

"I think we're almost there," said Libby as she placed a three-pegged, one-holed piece in the upper right corner.

"I think so, too," I said.

❖   ❖   ❖

One week before closing, Marshall's strapping brother Dave visited us. Dave was one year younger than Marshall and looked exactly like him—only taller and lankier, with a mischievous glint in his eye. I'd hung out with him once before, during New Year's 2010, when we'd done the bonding thing. Together, we'd gushed about Marshall, each other, and relationships (which was both easier and more difficult to do while taking shots of tequila).

During Dave's San Francisco visit, I'd been tirelessly campaigning for his approval, planning a series of outings to keep him reeling in tourist-activity overdrive. On his last day, we were headed to Alcatraz, the former federal prison and national park—something Dave had been itching to see. I'd even managed to get my hot green hands on special ferry tickets, courtesy of *Wicked* company manager Tanase, which meant VIP boarding in a separate line. It was the final feather in my "Let me impress you so that you might like me" cap, since the *Official Siblings and Significant Others Guidebook* clearly stated that Dave would have to grant me official clearance before I was, in bro-to-bro terms, Totally Cool.

Monday night, we began our sunset ferry ride from Pier 33 through the frigid, choppy waters, circling the island as we approached.

"Classic Michael Bay wraparound shot," Marshall said. "Classic Mike," Dave agreed. Yes, conversation on the ferry consisted of my listening to the Roy Boys comment on and quote that movie *The Rock*, then banter more generally in their special hybrid language made up of semi-ironic spy talk and macho jargon (including "downloading intel" to mean "checking email" and "guns" to mean "muscles").

Finally, we arrived on the Rock for its spooky night tour—the last of the day. Once inside, we opted for its audio guide, which featured real inmates and guards talking about their experiences those many years ago.

Stationed on a 22-acre island in the middle of the Bay, Alcatraz had been one of the most infamous federal prisons of all time. In its day, it housed the criminals' criminals—the über-bad boys who had worn out their welcomes elsewhere. Closed in 1963,

Alcatraz had reopened for the past couple of decades as a museum and truly righteous tourist trap.

Together with our tour group, Marshall, Dave, and I stalked up and down the first cellblock lane, peering through the bars at the abandoned cells. Some were empty, while some had been set up to look as they might have back in the day: inhabited by prisoners years into their sentences.

"Pretty cool, right?" I said to Dave, as our footsteps echoed off the concrete.

"It's totally the best," he said, at which point I mentally fist-pumped with myself.

I am so Totally Cool.

We walked on. Moonlight seeped through the barred windows while clusters of bulbs dimly lit the way. When we reached a new aisle, I squinted to examine a plaque on the wall, which hung in front of a cell. It described favorite prisoner pastimes and, accordingly, the display included an easel, an assortment of drawing implements, cards, and a board game that looked like Checkers. Prisoners would pass the time, the plaque said, confined to a small space, where they tried to amuse themselves through hours of boredom.

Ha!

A few paces more, and I turned to Marshall, who had wedged his face between two metal bars. I tapped his shoulder, relaying my Eureka moment.

"Just like a standby!"

"I was going to say the same thing!" he said, giving me a palm-burning high five.

"I've got to text Libby."

Nearby, Dave was creeping into an open cell. Soon, Marshall had joined him, and they started snapping photos of each other on the tiny cell toilet, while I got a text back from my wife:

Libby: 7:21PM youre so insane!

We continued around the bend and through the prisoner cafeteria, while I smiled in self-satisfied glee. I felt so clever to have drawn such a darkly funny conclusion:

Standbys are like prisoners! Chortle, chortle.

Next, we neared a solitary confinement cell. Through my headphones, a former inmate described the psychological challenges of spending so much time in isolation. In total darkness, he would throw a coin in the air, wait for the clinking sound of it hitting the ground, then scramble to find it. This he did, over and over, to ease the pain of loneliness and monotony.

Chortle, chortle?

This wasn't funny.

Even if I'd felt alone sometimes—reeling from the challenges *Wicked* presented me—it had never *really* been the case. No, not at all. I thought of Marshall. Then Libby. And Etai. Nic, Neka, and the whole game night crew. And, of course, Eden. My coworkers; my friends. None of us was ever alone.

At the end of the tour, we looped back and exited to the grounds, passing the residential buildings that had once held the prison guards and their wives and children. Their lives (the tour explained) were actually comfortable, albeit isolated. Here, surrounded by water, they had formed their own little community, ferrying into the city to go to school, gather supplies, and reintegrate with the rest of civilization.

I thought of the rest of the *Wicked* cast, all of whom had family, friends, and lives outside of San Francisco. We had shared a singular experience—one that had never been, and would never be again. Together, it seemed, we had lived on our own island.

On an island of Wicked.

As we waited in line to re-board and head back to the mainland, I thought of my own family back east. How were they doing, now that my grandmother was gone? How were my parents? And my sister, now that she was applying to colleges? What was "real life" like, since I'd catapulted over the rainbow?

What would it be like to go back?

A twilight glow lingered over the choppy ocean. I realized that the days here in Oz had blurred together as one long stretch of time—somehow separate and in a different universe, spinning on its own axis.

In doing *Wicked*, I had taken steps toward a new future. Now that I was on the brink of returning home, my future felt as unlimited as ever. I remembered my rehearsals with Bryan.

What is an unlimited future?

Not bound by conventional strictures, by the shackles that have always held me back.

As I felt the ferry rock and cradle me, I glanced over at Marshall who, against a backdrop of the cloudy night sky, was debating with Dave over which was the better aircraft: a helicopter or a zeppelin.

Becky's words echoed in my head.

"You and Marshall are not *you and Matt."*

He'd seemed too good to be true. But he *had* come true.

So much had.

I had played Elphaba. Not just once—*over forty times*.

I had forged a lifelong friendship—and learned that you can't judge a standby's book by her sparkly cover.

I had learned how to live far away from home.

I had learned to deal with tremendous loss, of a loved one and of a piece of home itself.

I had learned how to let go of past losses.

I had yanked back the curtain to see the formidable Wizard of Theater, examining him as he pushed buttons, pulled levers, and tugged his vast network of strings.

Here in Oz, I had learned what it meant to be *green*, inside and out, as I fumbled my way to becoming a professional actor.

So, what would happen next?

I knew better than to try to predict the future. But still, I just wanted to *know*.

Would there still be time for dreaming?

❖   ❖   ❖

On closing night, we all wore our evening best. For Libby, this meant a short black number; for Neka, a blue and black floor-length gown topped by a Jennifer Lopez updo, circa 2007; for me, a spandex dress with a rooster's tail that had looked much cuter in the store's skinny mirrors.

"I'm going to miss you, girl," said Neka, batting her ridiculously long lashes at me.

"Then there'd better be major double-dating in our future," I said, "or at least treadmill trotting."

"Come visit me in L.A.," said Neka, drifting out the door and into the girls' dressing room.

"I definitely will!" I called after her, hoping this would be true, silently wishing her the best.

On this, the last night, many of us had exchanged cards or goodbye post-its. I myself had Photoshopped famous works of art so they looked green (the Statue of David, the Mona Lisa, the Birth of Venus) and handed them out in little envelopes. I, of course, took special care to write Libby a long, sappy, "I love you forever and ever" note, with hearts and stars drawn around the perimeter.

Together, she and I watched the company's final performance from the back of the mezzanine, where we hugged and shed many sloppy tears. Neither of us was a parent, but we decided the experience was like saying goodbye to our problem child after he went away to college. Sure, we'd miss him—the tickle fights, the gold star book reports—but we certainly wouldn't miss shuttling him to soccer practice, meeting him in the principal's office, or force-feeding him vegetables.

He was a grown up now.

And we had the rest of our lives to live.

When the show ended, Libby and I joined the company onstage. Together we stood, holding hands through the applause, and took one final bow.

CURTAIN CALL.
RETURN TO KANSAS

ɛ౧

GREEN

/grin/ *adjective*

10. full of life and vigor: *green in heart.*

20. TRANSITION

September 6, 2010. Felicia's Blog.

Wicked closed last night. How do I describe my feelings?

Some folks asked me if I was sad, and I'd have to say no—but with a giant, multifaceted asterisk. I am sad insofar as something beautiful that was, no longer is; and that's a huge loss to deal with.

But *Wicked*'s closing also evokes so much positive emotion, as I think of all the lives it's touched here in San Francisco. I know (from your letters and kind words at the stage door, to my own personal experience) that the story of *Wicked* is timeless, inspirational, cathartic, and quite universal—and I think I would be much sadder if its message had never been disseminated. I'm thrilled to see firsthand how it has worked its magic on literally hundreds of thousands of people—and I'm thrilled to have been a part of it.

Bottom line? Thank you! Thank you, *Wicked*; thank you, amazing fans; thank you, universe; thank you, Mom and Dad; thank you everybody who came together to make this life-changing experience possible.

On the bright side: now I get to paint my nails any color I want.

Today, I choose purple!

Marshall's and my flight was scheduled to leave the morning after closing. We squared away our apartment, emptying the pantry, cleaning every last crevice—taking down the "set" we'd mounted for our extended bid of playing house. Now there was only an air mattress in the corner, on which we lay in the early morning blackness.

Neither of us could sleep. We were too wide-eyed from the closing night party and the excitement of returning to New York.

New York.

City where we'd met. City where we'd soon return.

"Did you ever think this day would come?" I asked.

"I feel like I've been living in San Francisco for years," said Marshall. He looked over at me, then added, "No offense, or anything."

"None taken."

"You're really awesome to live with," he said.

"You, too," I said.

When all was said and done, we'd spent nearly the whole of our relationship in Oz. What would it be like to ship ourselves back?

Would it be like getting in a time machine and hitting the rewind button?

Just as I wondered who I would be without *Wicked*, so did I wonder what kind of couple we'd be without San Francisco. Despite our whining about the weather, the lack of transportation, and the crack pipes on our street, it *had* become our home.

On the air mattress we lay awake, our pinkies touching. After a few minutes, I rolled over and said,

"Do you want to, like, go to the airport right now?"

Marshall thought about this for a few moments.

"Yeah, duh," he said.

So we lugged down our suitcases, called a cab, and bid farewell to our apartment. The gates didn't open until 4 a.m., so we sat in plastic seats near the airport's sliding doors, watching movies on my computer.

Hadn't I been here before?

In a flash, I saw the neon green walls of the terminal-like casting office, where all of this had begun. There, I'd dawdled in limbo, waiting to be called in for my audition.

Was I in limbo once more?

(LL101: **Just wait and see.**)

SFO to NYC

Back to reality.

21. GAME SHOW INTERLUDE, OR, A WHIMSICAL DEVICE THAT CONVEYS THE PASSAGE OF TIME AND CLARIFIES THIS BOOK'S MAJOR THEMES

HOST: *Welcome back to the final round of What the Heck Should I Do With My Life—the game show that lets you make life-changing decisions! This week's contestant is none other than Felicia Ricci, the newly professional actress who went about her unnaturally green way standing by for Elphaba in the San Francisco company of* Wicked. *Well, she's back, folks! Back in New York City, ready for some serious soul-searching. Let's give her a round of applause!*

(Crowd goes wild.)

FELICIA: *Thanks for having me. Although I must say, I'm not thrilled to be here.*

HOST: *Well, you don't have much of a choice. Our random selection process means contestants don't always get to choose whether or not they're on the show. Consider yourself lucky!*

FELICIA: Okay.

HOST: Let's get right down to things. Felicia, you've always been a bit of a dreamer, am I right?

FELICIA: Guilty as charged.

(Crowd hisses.)

HOST: All right, all right, let's not hold it against her. When you first got cast in Wicked, you thought realizing a dream would answer some big questions for you. That the "greenness" of your life experience would somehow fade, and you would grow into a new phase of clarity, certainty, and accomplishment. Am I right?

FELICIA: Uh, I guess I didn't know it at the time, but yeah, I think that sums it up.

HOST: Now, to fill in our viewers at home—what happened there? Where did it go wrong?

FELICIA: Uh, well, with all due respect, I wouldn't necessarily say it went wrong—

HOST: Then when did you stop trying? When did you pull away and fold under the pressure?

FELICIA: I don't think I did either! My only problem is that I still have questions. Questions that I thought would get answered.

HOST: Questions?!

(Crowd boos.)

FELICIA: *Hear me out! It's just that a lot of people I know in theater seem certain about what they want to do. But I'm not. So I thought, well? There must be something wrong.*

HOST: *You are absolutely correct. When it comes to deciding who you are and what to do with your life, you need to settle on one thing—and stick to it! Anything less makes for too much confusion, both for you— and your audience. They want a satisfying narrative arc, am I right?*

(Crowd cheers.)

FELICIA: *But settling on one way to describe myself to the audience would be lying.*

HOST: *But isn't lying for the sake of a pat ending so much more fun than reality?*

(HOST turns to crowd. They cheer louder.)

FELICIA: *But—I'm torn. I want the audience to trust me but at the same time, I don't want to leave them without some grand, satisfying ending that delivers them the clarity I keep searching for myself.*

HOST: *Well, Felicia—now's your chance! Now that you've reached the final round of What the Heck Should I Do With My Life, you get to choose where your path will next take you after* Wicked. *Are you ready?*

FELICIA: *Uh?*

HOST: *Aw, c'mon now! Somebody's a 'fraidy pants!*

(Crowd starts to heckle. "Get a grip!" "Quit your whining!" "Give it up!")

FELICIA: I'm sorry.

HOST: Hasn't it all come down to this moment? Since Wicked, *haven't you been searching for answers? For a decision on what to do next?*

FELICIA: Sure, I guess.

HOST: Then it's time to decide if professional theater is the right path for you!

FELICIA: When you put it that way, then, I guess, okay.

HOST: You heard her, folks. It's time…to choose!

(Crowd goes wild.)

HOST: According to the official What the Heck Should I Do With My Life *rules, once you spin the wheel, you have to follow through with whatever the arrow lands on. No "ifs" "and" or "buts." It's total commitment from here on out. Do you think you can do that?*

FELICIA: That sounds like the opposite of how life really works.

HOST: …Which is why this is such a great game! No more uncertainty, Felicia. Just a future, clear and bright. A yellow brick road, straight and narrow.

FELICIA: Have you been stealing metaphors from my memoir?

HOST: We're still in your memoir, Felicia.

FELICIA: Oh, that is super weird.

HOST: Can we bring out the Future Wheel?

(Crowd cheers, then hushes, as the Future Wheel is rolled out by two leggy ladies in sequined jumpers.)

HOST: This is it, Felicia. The moment of truth.

(Crowd starts thumping their feet on the risers.)

HOST: Here on our Wheel we have: (1) Actress, (2) Housewife, (3) Writer, (4) Salaried Office Worker (with Benefits!), or (5) Unemployed Deadbeat.

FELICIA: Wait—isn't there some kind of hybrid option? Where you can combine, say, two of the four? Or tackle each of them, one at a time?

HOST: Not the way certainty works, sweetie.

FELICIA: Can I make a pro-con chart, or something? To really figure out what is best?

HOST: Why bother? That's why we have the Future Wheel. To decide for you!

(Crowd cheers.)

FELICIA: Can't I at least spin a few times, see where it lands, and split the difference? I thought that was an option?

(FELICIA panders to crowd for support. They boo.)

HOST: *You couldn't be more wrong.*

FELICIA: *But, isn't it—? Hey, is Life Lessons 101 in the audience? Life Lessons 101, back me up here!*

(Silence from the crowd. Somebody coughs. A baby cries.)

HOST: *But what does Life Lessons 101 know, anyway? Nevermind that touchy-feely, keep-an-open-mind, life-is-fluid nonsense. This is Life Lessons 201. Welcome to higher learning!*

(Crowd starts chanting, "Spin it, spin it, spin it!")

HOST: *You know what they want. You know what you want. Now go ahead. SPIN!*

(Felicia steps forward, takes a deep breath, and spins the Future Wheel.)

22. BACK TO SQUARE 101

As the Host said in our bizarre Game Show Interlude, you, dear reader, deserve a conclusion. Something that inspires you to venture forth, soldiering into your own unnaturally green adventure!

This, my friend, I cannot give you.

I can, however, submit an account of what happened next—the recent and curious events that led me here, to this moment, as I physically type words on the page.

(Hi, future reader! It's me, Felicia, from the past! TIME TRAVEL THROUGH BOOKS!)

When my production closed, *Wicked* San Francisco didn't (as I once imagined) evaporate—poof!—in a blink. Instead, it slowly receded into the past, where it remains a living memory—one I revisit often.

Its people, of course, live on, kicking and doing jazz hands on all corners of the globe. After *Wicked,* Neka was reunited with Nic on the *Mary Poppins* tour, where they "step in time" together and post blissful Facebook photos of their cross-country adventures. Our shoulder-grabbing friend Etai is now playing Boq on Broadway, along with the famously toned-armed Teal, and Tom, my fun-loving Wizard. The lovely and talented Libby is making waves in the New York theater scene, charming the best of them (as she charmed me, those many-odd months go). She and I still see each other often—squealing, gushing, and engaging in other slumber party frivolity.

As for me?

Oh, how I wish I could sum up my life in one sentence.

Felicia Ricci lived happily ever after, with pit stains.

Here is what I do know.

After September 5, I started writing everyday—in between theater auditions, workshops, and concerts. Journals. Blogs. Story outlines.

Slowly, the idea for this memoir took shape, and I began a book-writing adventure that is now just shy of one year in the making. This adventure reawakened the English major in me, my love of writing, and my long-harbored sense of curiosity.

The questions resurfaced, in droves.

Who was I after *Wicked*?

What kind of a career could I have?

What is a career? Is it just one thing?

When should I shut up and stop asking questions?

I'd heard murmurs of this kind of uncertainty for nearly all my life. *Wicked*, I had thought, would be my answer. But it only led to more questions.

What does it mean to be unlimited?

As you might expect, the questioning got me into a bit of a career tangle, at which point I impulsively spun my Future Wheel, deciding it was time to retry my hand at a "Salaried Office Job (with Benefits!)" since I needed some kind of steady income while I wrote my book.

So, I got a job writing for a downtown wedding magazine, where I had my own cubicle and everything.

At first I was excited.

This is just like a chick lit novel!

I soon realized that this was a misapprehension on my part since nothing about the job was at all witty, amusing, or overrun with banter and quippy observations about striking out in the big city.

In the end, not only did Salaried Office Job (with Benefits!) fail to answer my questions, it raised a million more.

With a full-time job, could theater remain a part of my life?

Could I be creative, and still make a living?

I was thrust into an extended bout of Freshman Year of Life déjà vu.

All I kept thinking was, *What's the deal, Life Lessons 101? I thought I would have graduated by now.*

Why was I still so *green*?

In the midst of this questioning, I knew I needed some help.

I needed to get back to my roots.

So I enrolled in a class.

(A familiar one, with a familiar title.)

⁘   ⁘   ⁘

"In the real world, a mom might tell a kid, 'No, you can't have that pony.' But here you say, '*Yes*, you can have that pony, *and* here's the man who's going to sell it to us.' See how that works?" Mike's forehead was flush from the heat. He was gesticulating with both hands, a man in the throes of teaching passion. "'Yes, And' is the driving principle behind all improvisation. Use 'Yes, And' to work with your scene partner and get on the same page."

We all nodded, wide-eyed.

It was my first day in Improv 101 at the Upright Citizen's Brigade, a famous New York theater and training center that had birthed dozens of comedy greats. Mike, our red-bearded teacher, was a comedian-about-town and one of UCB's best improvisers. He appeared many times each week on their dilapidated stage, sweating and yelling like a big, charismatic Viking.

"All right, let's get two people up."

Today our goal wasn't to be funny, but merely to apply improv's core principle of "Yes, And." The exercise was literally to say "yes," repeat back what your scene partner had just said, then add the next piece of information ("and").

Yes, it sounded simple—*And* yet I was terrified.

What the heck would I do without a script?

Two boys volunteered to start us off, and began doing a scene about alligator hunting. Even though it was the most terrible scene I'd ever witnessed, I couldn't help but chuckle. Inside our classroom, humor was contagious; our laughter emanated from a place of support, not judgment.

In Life Lessons 101—er, Improv 101—we were all giving it our best shot.

"All right, let's get two more people up."

I rose from my seat and took to the floor, my blouse drenched in sweat, my heart performing a drum solo in multiple time signatures. Next to me stood Whitney, my soon-to-be scene partner, a short-haired sparkplug who over-enunciated everything in a Southern drawl.

"Okay, can I get a location, please?" said Mike. "Where are Whitney and Felicia?"

"In the womb," said Nicola, a bird-like woman with a pan-European accent.

In the womb? What?

"Take it away."

Not knowing what the hell was going on, I curled next to Whitney and pressed my cupped hands against my chest. (You know, the way fetuses do.)

"Hi, sister," said Whitney.

"Yes, hi, sister," I replied.

So far, so good.

"I, um, I don't know. What gender are we?"

I am the worst improviser ever.

"Okay, hang on," said Mike, raising a hand.

"Yeah, sorry," I said—relieved to be called out as Le Suck.

"No, no, don't apologize. I was just going to say that in improv, if you ask questions, it's not going far enough. It's kind of cheating, because you're asking your partner to fill in the blanks for you. In improv, the question is the thing that leads you to a statement. Skip the question, and tell us the answer."

I wish I knew the answer, I thought.

We reset to our two-fetus clump, to start the scene again.

A few months before, when I'd taken my Salaried Office Job (with Benefits!), I'd self-imposed a break from theater. I didn't know why, entirely. But I'd felt uncertain—and that was okay.

After some time, I felt ready again. For something.

"Hi, sister," Whitney said again.

"Yes...hi sister," I repeated back. "I, um, am a girl. And that is my gender."

"Yes, you are a girl, and it sure is hot in here."

Scattered chuckles from the class.

"Yes, it *is* hot in here," I said, gesturing to my sticky pits, "and I think I hear a rumbling sound!"

"Yes, there's a rumbling sound! And I think it's because Mom ate something spicy."

Or, duh, she's in labor, I thought.

"Yes, you think it's because Mom ate something spicy, but it could be something else," I said.

"You're saying no!" hollered Mike. "Whitney says it's because Mom ate something spicy, so that's the truth. Say 'yes!'" Mike's face was bright red, his whiskers the color of burning wheat.

"Right! Sorry about that," I said to my fetus-sister.

Don't say no!

His words reverberated in my head.

By spinning the Future Wheel I'd tried to understand who I was by closing doors—as if identity were a mere process of elimination.

Really it was the opposite.

Don't say no.

I was struck by the irony: doing professional theater had shown me that I could do anything—so while theater might be one path, it might not be the *only* path. Or at least, it didn't *have* to be. If *Wicked* hadn't instilled in me the certainty I'd wanted, it had nudged me to reconsider my so-called yellow brick road— other exits, other routes, other ways of being *me*.

"Mom ate something spicy," I said, "and I think I smell *taquitos*."

"Yes, you smell *taquitos*, and we should do something about it."

"Yes, we should do something about it." I paused to consider. "Let's kick her!"

We thrust our legs high into the air, laughing our braying fetus laughs as we kicked our imaginary mother in the imaginary uterus.

As I did, I felt like I was knocking down a big, menacing door.

I would say Yes, And.

Yes to being myself.

And to being green.

(**GREEN.** 10. full of life and vigor: *green in heart.*)

❖   ❖   ❖

A month after returning from San Francisco, I made the official move to Marshall's Brooklyn apartment. With me I brought all my stuff, plus some furniture Grandma Yola had left behind. Together, we shuffled the pieces around, scooting her couch into the living room right next to her armchair, and placing her little avocado-colored cabinet in the center of our kitchen. When all was in place, we ordered pizza. Instead of eating it on the floor, we sat at our table. Instead of paper plates, we used flatware.

"This will be our third apartment together," Marshall said.

"Let's not move for a while," I replied.

I didn't think we would—even though there'd be work to do. Without a dishwasher or storage closets, we'd have to redraft our Living Together Treaty. Already, the protein bins had commandeered the far corner of the kitchen, and with his new personal trainer job in Manhattan, Marshall would be keeping ungodly hours.

But I had a good feeling. My grandma's furniture felt cozy and warm, just like the rest of it.

Marshall reached his hand toward me.

"Oh, you've got some—"

"Food on my face?"

I took a napkin and swiped it all the way from my forehead to my chin.

"No, actually," Marshall said. "Green, behind your ear."

He took his napkin, dipped it in his water glass, and reached for me.

"Still?" I said, as he dabbed it off.

"Still."

~~THE END~~

TO BE CONTINUED

ACKNOWLEDGMENTS

I wrote in my blog that it takes a village to raise an Elphaba; the same applies to this book. To my readers: you guys *rock so hard!* A million hugs and kisses for your kind words and well-wishes. Thank you to my amazing editors (and main characters) Gentle Rambo Marshall and best friend Becky, without whose insight and close reading I would be lost. (Sidebar: Look out for best friend Becky, a.k.a. Rebecca Harrington's brilliant novel in the fall of 2012.) Much gratitude to Annie Jacobson, my photographer and design consultant; to my superhuman copyeditor Elisabeth Ness; and to Lisa Scottoline and Francesca Serritella, who encourage and inspire me daily with their writerly genius and determination.

Hats off to the team at *Wicked* who, for whatever reason, decided to take a chance on a wide-eyed, pit-stained gal like me. And a massive "thank you" to all my delightful characters. On the page, you were a joy to write; off the page, you remain wonderful friends. Special shout-out to David Lober, who provided me with a source doc of all our text messages. (Is he an amazing stage manager, or what?)

Finally, I must return to my sources, including dictionary.com for supplying my *green* definitions, and Patricia and Anthony Ricci for supplying me with, well, life. I thank them for their unconditional support as I continue down this yellow brick road less traveled, poking fun at their affinity for Italian food and quoting them hyperbolically.

And, of course, there's Yola—the original baller G. I love you, Gram. Forever and ever.

Made in the USA
San Bernardino, CA
25 November 2012